# The Mindset of a Champion: Your Favorite Rapper's Least Favorite Book

BYRON CRAWFORD

Copyright © 2013 Byron Crawford

All rights reserved.

ISBN: 1478330929
ISBN-13: 978-1478330929

# DEDICATION

This book is dedicated to Donda West, Pimp C, Philant Johnson, Aaliyah, Charles Hamilton, Proof from D-12, VIBE magazine, DJ AM and that dog I killed when I was 17.

# CONTENTS

|  | Acknowledgments | i |
|---|---|---|
| 1 | There's No Such Thing as a Free Newspaper | 1 |
| 2 | How All Got Started Way Back When | 8 |
| 3 | A Mind Is a Terrible Thing to Waste | 13 |
| 4 | Post-Graduate Work (at White Castle) | 16 |
| 5 | Ban Kanye West from the Grammys | 21 |
| 6 | Don't Hate Free Speech, Hate Yourself | 29 |
| 7 | That Wasn't Not Funny | 38 |
| 8 | Best Week Ever | 46 |
| 9 | Career Opportunities | 49 |
| 10 | Puppet Show and Ghostface | 58 |
| 11 | I Am the Leprechaun | 63 |
| 12 | Standing on Top of Hip-Hop Journalism | 72 |
| 13 | Another Man's Freedom Fighter | 81 |
| 14 | Damn, Gina! | 91 |
| 15 | Short People Got No Reason to Live | 104 |
| 16 | Addition by Subtraction | 114 |
| 17 | Fanute Bol | 123 |

# ACKNOWLEDGMENTS

Thank you to everyone I had to step on on my way to the top.

# 1 THERE'S NO SUCH THING AS A FREE NEWSPAPER

Never let it be said that nothing good ever came out of 9/11. I started blogging a few weeks after 9/11, after I read an article in the USA Today about how people were using blogs to document their experiences on that day, their thoughts on the upcoming wars in Iraq and Afghanistan, and what have you.

I didn't used to read USA Today on the reg, obvs, it just happened to be sitting there on the table where I was having breakfast. I could have gotten up and grabbed another paper, but you know how it is in the morning, when you haven't had your coffee. USA Today is a good newspaper for when your mind isn't 100%.

There were newspapers lying around all over the place at the school I went to, East Bumblefuck State University in Chicken Switch, MO, a/k/a Josephine Baker State University, a/k/a the Harvard of the Midwest, a/k/a the teachers college (which is what Chicken Switch natives called it), because the school took part in one of those scams in which the student body was compelled beyond its will to provide a huge subsidy to the dying newspaper industry, and in exchange the students all received free subscriptions to any two newspapers of our choosing, from a list of about five total.

Most semesters I went with the New York Times and the St. Louis Post-

Dispatch, from my native St. Louis (duh). The Post-Dispatch was good for staying abreast of local news and events, on the outside chance that anything happened in St. Louis. The New York Times, for all of its flaws, is an enjoyable newspaper to read. I especially enjoyed the op-ed page and the arts section.

At least one semester I was stuck having to subscribe to the Wall Street Journal, because I was in one of those classes where you had to bring in the day's Wall Street Journal and discuss various articles you were supposed to have read. I was a business major. I never read so much as a word of the Wall Street Journal, but I couldn't just show up to class without a newspaper tucked under my arm. That would have been a dead giveaway.

I already had something along the lines of a blog. It was something I put together for a class called Business Computer Applications.

Business Computer Applications was the class they make you take during Freshman Week if you're a business major. It was only one credit hour, and it only met for half a semester, plus Freshman Week. Even that may have been longer than necessary, given what we did in this class.

We were taught basic things like how to access information via the Internets, how to set up an email address, how to send and receive email, so on and so forth. Keep in mind, this was still the 1990s. There either wasn't a such thing as Google, or most people hadn't heard of it yet. Many of the kids at this school came from the sticks and had probably never used a computer.

First day of class, all we did was watch that movie where Joe Pesci plays a homeless guy who audits a class at Harvard, on VHS. There's a good Madonna song on the soundtrack. It plays over the end credits, as I recall.

Second day of class, I showed up a little bit late (I know...), and no one was there. I didn't know what the fuck was going on. It was like that scene in Vanilla Sky where they cleared out all of the cars and people from Times Square. Had college somehow been canceled?

Walking back to my dorm room, I was reminded that there was a field trip to a lake. I didn't know how to get to the lake, so I couldn't just show up in my car. I had to go back to my dorm room and play with my computer. I'd have to catch up with them later, in the afternoon. When they got back from the lake, they were going on a walking tour of downtown, which was all of about one square block and was mostly boarded up. It looked like a sadder version of the downtown area in the movie The Tree of Life.

I headed downtown on foot and ran into my class on the way into a coffee shop. It was like a Starbucks but with random religious shit all over the place. The town wasn't big enough for a real Starbucks to come along and run this place out of business. Alas. Ironically enough, I was the only one who had any coffee. As was the case with the Internets, these kids had yet to get up on drinking coffee.

I started drinking coffee when I was 15. You're not supposed to drink coffee as a kid, because it stunts your growth, but that wasn't as much of a concern for me personally. If I hadn't developed a six cup a day habit barely out of middle school, it's possible I would have grown to be 10 feet tall and 600 pounds. If I had it to do over, I would have started drinking coffee at age four.

Later that week, we were taught how to make basic web pages using Notepad and, like, four lines worth of HTML. I never knew it was so easy. The assignment was to create a page with your name on it, your email address, some Playboy Questionnaire-like personal information and maybe some shitty clip art. If you knew anyone else with an email address, you could send them a link to it. I'm not sure if it was possible to find these pages using a search engine. The technology may not have been sophisticated enough just yet.

A few weeks later, into the actual school year, I got the bright idea to go back and add several things to my web page. Things that wouldn't have been as appropriate for a classroom setting. But nothing too out there. Some of it was just irrelevant. It's a testament to my thought process and perhaps my understanding of technology at the time that I didn't just create a separate page on which I could have written anything I wanted to. The class was damn near over anyway. I'd already received an A for the assignment. It was one of the very best things I turned in the entire time I was in college.

I'd go back and update it every now and again, if something interesting happened to me. Like, if I went to a fast food restaurant and ate an especially good sandwich, or one of my cousins broke out of prison—the kind of things I might have otherwise written about in an email cc'd to eight or 10 guys I went to high school with. Kids don't do that anymore, do they? I guess that's what Facebook is for.

Tucker Max started out emailing people about—spoiler alert—times he got really drunk and banged chicks. If I'd had what it takes to make sweet, passionate love to more (or any) women, perhaps I could have had a similar career... le sigh.

One year I got stuck living with this African kid. He was good for a few stories.

My first three roommates all had to move out after a semester or two, but not because there's anything wrong with me. They just had to go live somewhere else.

The first guy spent too much time playing a game called Everquest and had to drop out. He stopped going to classes a few weeks into the semester, but he stuck around for a while after that, because the school had very fast Internets in those days, and I guess his room and board was already paid for. They don't prorate it if you drop out. But then some tweakers broke into his car and stole his CD player, and he became afraid and bitter.

The second guy was a football player from Arizona. He was as big as I was, i.e. larger than a mofo, and he hardly seemed any more athletic. But this was a Division II school. You had to be close enough to the players to see their mustaches to know it wasn't a high school team. Size was everything. I would have gone out for the football team, but what good would it have done? Believe it or not, I went to college on a full academic scholarship. There was a time in my life when I had potential.

This guy from Arizona was the guy who put me up on the Gin Blossoms' excellent New Miserable Experience, which I can't recommend highly enough. He grew up in the same town they were from and saw them live back in the day. So jealous... We downloaded a few of their songs from Napster, along with random songs that leaked from great albums like

Ghostface Killah's Supreme Clientele, and Eminem's The Marshall Mathers LP, and "3 AM" by Matchbox 20, which we would listen to every night at "3 AM." No homo.

He moved into a house with some other guys from the football team, and I ended up moving in with this guy I sorta kinda knew from—I'm not too proud to admit—the school marching band, the Showboat Gamblers, in which I played tuba. He was a big fan of the group Fuel. (He may have been the only one.) He even had a haircut similar to lead singer Brett Scallions, but that may have just been a coincidence. I've to really appreciate the song "Shimmer," which is one of the very best songs of the '90s, but this was around the time the album with the song "Hemorrhage in My Hands" came out, and I wasn't a very big fan.

One time I vomited on a pile of his clothes, he seemed annoyed that I would watch cable news at all hours of the day and night (pre-George W. Bush, mind you), and I would have a look at his girlfriend's ass on the reg, but I don't think any of that had to do with him moving out. I think some guys he may or may not have been related to were getting a house.

I called the girl who was in charge of the residence halls to find out what my options were, since my roommate was moving out at the semester. She said there were more rooms available than kids who wanted to live in the dorms, and since it was the middle of the school year, I could probably get the room to myself without having to pay the additional fee they charge to get a room to yourself. Bonus. I went home for winter break thinking I had come up.

She must have thought I was white. Sometimes I don't sound as black as I need to sound over the phone, because I grew up in a nice area. Otherwise she wouldn't have toyed with my emotions like that. Black kids who don't have anyone else to live with often get stuck living with these African kids the school has shipped in Mariel Boatlift-style as part of another one of their scams, this one to make it seem as if the student body is 3% black.

I'd always wondered about that. It says in the EBSU brochure that the school is 3% black, but you get to a certain point, after you've been there a year or so, where you know every other black kid in the entire school on a first name basis, and there's only like eight of them. There's about 5,000 students total and maybe 3,500 undergrad. I can't do that kind of math without a calculator, but you'd think that 3% of 5,000, or even 3,500, would be more than eight.

The balance of the student population, i.e. the other 97%, was almost all white. There must have been less than 1% "other," i.e. various kinds of Asians and what have you. Hispanics. Native American Indians. You'd think that would make it that much easier for a brother such as myself to stand out academically, but a lot of those white kids were madd smart. If it weren't for affirmative action, or, more likely, a shedload of Asian and Jewish kids, they could have gone to a school someone actually heard of.

EBSU had been designated as Missouri's only "highly selective" public school. I'm not sure what exactly that meant, or how it benefited me personally, but in effect it meant that the school couldn't just admit any ol' dumbass. The average ACT score hovered up around 30, and as they liked to point out, even on the football team it was 27. They couldn't just admit black kids from here in Missouri without throwing off the average. If the average fell too low, the administration might have had to take a pay cut. God forbid.

And so taxpayer money that, theoretically, could have been used to do a better job educating black kids here in the US was used to fly African kids halfway around the world and put them up, free of charge, in what to them must have been roughly the equivalent of the Waldorf-Astoria, with all you can eat cafeteria food (albeit made by the same company that makes prison food), and huge, corn-fed white women as far as the eye can see.

President Obama's father, Barack Obama, Sr., was brought over as part of a similar program in the 1950s. He even got to go to school in Hawaii. Who even knew there was a college in Hawaii? I didn't bother applying to any schools outside of Missouri, because I was raised to have low expectations. Obama the elder must have had higher test scores than the African kids who get stuck at, say, some random former directional school out near the Missouri-Iowa border.

It was revealed in CIA documents recently released under the Freedom of

Information Act that Barack Obama, Sr. had to be sent back to Africa before he impregnated too many white women. Really, one was enough. After he knocked up the president's mother, he went off to Harvard for grad school, where he took up with another white chick. They pulled his visa before he could have any more kids—that we know of. I think he was already married with children over in Africa, but legally you're allowed to have different wives on different continents. (Look it up if you don't believe me.)

It was also revealed that the Asian guy the president's mother took up with after his real father got sent back to Africa was putting a shoe on her, when they were living in Indonesia. Though for all I know, that may have been allowed. As Mitt Romney likes to point out, they eat dogs in Indonesia. When in Rome.

# 2 HOW IT ALL GOT STARTED WAY BACK WHEN

The problem with having a blog, as opposed to a static web page, is that you have to update a blog a lot more frequently. (You really do have to.) At least once a day, if not several times a day. And it's not like something interesting happens to you that often. It's not every day that you have an especially good sandwich from a fast food restaurant, one of your relatives breaks out of prison, or your African roommate tries to convert you to Jehovah's Witness, to try to break you of your supposedly harmful pr0n habit.

I found myself in the same situation a lot of people are in when they start a blog. While it's true that there's literally six gozillion blogs on the Internets, the vast majority of them—pretty much all of them—consist of only a few posts: a post in which the author introduces himself; a post or two about what the author had for lunch; maybe a picture of some poor cat who didn't (and couldn't) consent to having its picture posted on the Internets, and that's about it. They haven't been updated since 2004.

I was able to deal with this issue in a couple of ways: (1) I copied and pasted text verbatim from a spam entertainment news newsletter I used to receive, a sort of email version of those '80s-era fax machine newsletters; (2) I made up a series of fake news stories about some of the special kids I went to high school with. The one eventually led to the other.

I would read something I found interesting in those spam emails, and I'd just copy and paste it into the text window of the software I used to update my blog, click publish, and voila! There was my post for the afternoon. It's Miller Time. I didn't realize that I was supposed to strategically rewrite the story in my own words, as if that somehow constitutes providing a worthwhile contribution to the Internets (that's how literally all Internets content is made), because I didn't have an example to follow. There weren't any other entertainment blogs back then. I invented the entertainment blog.

You know that scene in 2001: A Space Odyssey where one of those monkeys, our ancestors, realized that he could use one of the bones of a dead antelope to beat the shit out of the rest of the monkeys, thus securing more dead antelope meat for himself? Something similar happened to me in, wouldn't you know, the year 2001.

Most of the headlines in those spam emails weren't any good, because they were probably written by a room full of guys in India who don't know from American pop culture; they barely know English. (Yeah, I know India was once a British colony, and the most widely circulated English newspaper is from India, but bare with me. I'm making an important point here.) At a certain point, it occurred to me that I could write my own headlines, which were way better than anything they could write.

It started out with just adding a word here and there. A story about the late, great Whitney Houston would become a story about "Crackhead Whitney Houston." Then I started rewriting the headline altogether and leaving the body of the article copied and pasted verbatim. And then that went on for a while before I finally started rewriting entire articles (all four sentences) to make them more amusing to me personally.

One small step for man, one giant leap for mankind.

And this somehow evolved into writing stories of my own, out of whole cloth, about special kids I went to high school with.

I think the impetus for these stories was an article someone sent me about a guy who was the Head Punting Coach for my high school's football team (or maybe it was just a guy with the same name), who was sent to prison for embezzling money from a bank. I wanted to write about it, but it wasn't clear to me how in the hell this guy went from teaching high school kids how to kick a football (laces out!) to embezzling money from a bank. So of course I had to make something up.

Head Punting Coach isn't an actual position for which you can draw a salary from the school district, as far as I know. That was just a title he gave himself. His actual job was Professional Hall Monitor. Or maybe he was a full-time sub, and the kids just called him a Professional Hall Monitor, pejoratively.

I don't see what's so bad about being a professional hall monitor. The grade-level principals (not to be confused with the actual principal, known, I think, as Head Principal) essentially functioned as professional hall monitors. They'd stand in the hallway between classes and make sure the kids didn't beat each other up or do something sexually inappropriate. In retrospect, high school was a lot more like prison than I realized at the time. Dead Prez may have been on to something.

If you were a professional sub by trade, and you spent most of your time policing the hallways, if you didn't say anything, people might actually think you were some sort of administrator, rather than a glorified security guard, a/k/a toy cop. Whereas, I'm not even sure how one would become a full-time substitute teacher.

Regular substitute teachers, who work on a part-time, day to day basis, are people who went to college for like 12 years but they never could quite graduate, possibly because they can't read. Otherwise they'd just get a full-time teaching job. You don't have to have a degree in education in order to be a teacher, you just have to have graduated from college. It's like waitressing for the nominally educated. (According to Harvey Keitel in Reservoir Dogs, waitressing is the number one occupation for uneducated women. They rely on our tips to put food on their families.)

My parents have been trying to sucker me into to becoming a teacher ever since I graduated from college. Before that, when it wasn't clear that I definitely could graduate (pfft!), they were trying to get me to join the military. I think, on a certain level, they wanted me to go over to Iraq and get blown up by an IED. At least that way they could say their son died for his country. How do you explain to your friends that your son sits around all day in his underwear looking for pictures of certain kinds of girls on Tumblr?

However, it should be pointed out that the best schools are the most selective when it comes to hiring, and vice versa, obvs. Some of the teachers at the school I went to had Ph.Ds. But if you went into education because you're one of those who can't do, as the saying goes, you might get stuck working at a school in the hood. Which is of course mad dangerous. You're basically just there to call the cops if the students give each other a "buck 50," like Officer Pryzbylewski on The Wire. If you're an especially attractive woman, maybe you can inspire them to write essays on the civil rights movement.

Being a full-time substitute teacher is arguably preferable to being both the guy who works at Target and occasionally gets paid $40 to watch Shogun on VHS on his day off, i.e. a regular sub, and the guy who puts his life on the line every day warehousing hoodrats, until they're old enough to be funneled into the full-on prison-industrial complex. It must be reserved for people who were once popular athletes at the same school, who couldn't quite complete a degree in turf management.

And then there's the special kid who gets a job working in the school library. The high school I went to had a special kid who was given a sort of job working in the computer lab in the library.

This was after he kept coming back to school after they tried to graduate him, or "socially promote" him into adulthood, as it were. He would show up again the first day of the next school year. He didn't understand that "graduate" means you don't go to school anymore, and I guess his parents didn't have anything else to do with him. They'd try again, and he'd come right back. I personally witnessed him graduate from high school at least twice. I used to perform "Pomp and Circumstance" onstage at graduation. Don't tell anyone.

I guess finally, they figured they'd give him some sort of job. Scraping chewing gum from the undersides of desks using a razor blade would have been as demeaning as it was potentially dangerous. Local TV news would have eventually found out. The full-time subs were sometimes forced to set the porta potties out by the practice field back on their base after some vandal (me, admittedly) tipped them over, but they were ostensibly of normal intelligence.

Fortunately, he had somehow figured out how to launch Microsoft Word from the start menu in Windows 95. He was hanging out in the computer lab a lot anyway, because showing people how to do something made him feel superior. He'd be perched like an eagle, just waiting for someone who looked like they didn't know what they were doing. Then he'd pounce. Like, "Step aside and let the professional handle this!" Except I don't recall him being that verbose.

# 3 A MIND IS A TERRIBLE THING TO WASTE

Since no one read my blog, and since the content was so deeply asinine, it was nothing for me to put it on ice, so to speak, when I went home for the summer of '02. Not that I had anything else better to do. I'd hook up my old Super Nintendo, play Legend of Zelda: A Link to the Past and listen to Public Enemy. I liked to kick it old school. If I woke up in time, I'd listen to Howard Stern on 105.7 The Point.

As a lazy person who suffers from delusions of grandeur, it was easy to tell myself that I'd take a few months off, and then when I came back I'd be very ambitious. I wanted to do original writing on my beloved rap music. I wanted those great stories I was coming up with about special kids stealing each other's bicycles and punching out Fredbird at Special Kids Day at the Ballpark to be even more baroque. That spring, I purchased my own domain name, the one I still use to this day.

I don't think I need to tell you where this is going. That fall, I got back to school for what was either my second junior year or my first senior year, depending on how you look at it, and I focused on blogging for all of about two weeks. The spirit just wasn't the same. I felt like I was already over blogging. I was at risk of becoming one of those people who started a blog that they only ever updated four times.

And who knows, maybe I would have been, if I didn't have to spend an extra year college. Well, I guess I didn't have to. I could have just up and left when I realized I hadn't quite met the requirements to graduate. And I probably should have. Instead, I got suckered into sticking around for another year, thinking that if you graduate from college you make more money over the course of a lifetime. I fell victim to the propaganda.

Having been in college a full three years at that point, I was on track to have more or less the number of credit hours that I needed. I'd dropped a class here and there, but if I really buckled down and maybe picked up a class or two, I still could have hit whatever the magic number was at the end of four years. But it would have been all for naught, because my grades weren't the best in the world either. If you can imagine.

You only need a cumulative 2.0 in order to graduate, and I had that, easily. Even if I didn't, there's probably some basic literacy test you can take in order to receive a certificate stating that you did in fact spend at least four years in college. The president of the school board in Detroit, who's illiterate, tried to get one of those from Wa(y)ne State University, after being in college for 13 years, but he couldn't, because he couldn't pass the test, because he's illiterate. Duh. (He also got caught playing with himself during a school board meeting.)

Different departments at EBSU had different requirements in order to graduate with an actual degree in something. In order to graduate with a business degree, there were certain classes you had to take in the business department and elsewhere on campus, and you had to have at least a 3.0, i.e. a B average in your business classes. I didn't. I got a D in at least one business class and Cs in one or two others. I checked the stats, and my shit was off to the point where even if I aced what ended being my second junior year/first senior year, I still would have been off by a grade point or two. Fuuuuck.

If I had it to do over again, I would have taken the college equivalent of a GED and gone about my business. I only bothered trying to get that business degree because I figured no one would hire me with a general studies diploma. I didn't realize that no was gonna hire me anyway. I took another full year of college, more or less aced it, graduated with a business degree, and spent the next couple of years getting turned down for literally every quote-unquote real job there ever was. I've never been offered a job that paid more than about $8/hour. I am the 99%.

It was during my second senior year—my victory lap, as I like to call it—that I rededicated myself to blogging. My mind was sharp from having to put forth effort in class. No more drinking Natty Light by the case, starting at 12:30 in the afternoon. I had to wait until later in the evening. That was when I launched the current incarnation of my blog ByronCrawford.com: The Mindset of a Champion. I already had the domain name, from the last time I felt ambitious. It had yet to expire.

This time around I shifted my focus to writing things people might actually want to read: recaps of shows on MTV, years and years before it was all trendy, and humorous song by song reviews of rap albums.

And wouldn't you know, a few months later I had my first reader who wasn't someone I went to high school with that I emailed and told to read my site. I can't remember her name, but she was some hoodrat who was upset that I had made fun of Cam'ron. She probably fantasized about being one of those girls on his album skits giving him a blowski. Years later, when I met the legendary Combat Jack, he said he found my site looking for information on Cam'ron for a book he was writing about hip-hop jewelry. I got a lot of mileage out of writing about Cam'ron.

# 4 POST-GRADUATE WORK (AT WHITE CASTLE)

The week before I graduated from college, I called White Castle, where I'd been working on and off during breaks from school, to let them know that I'd be back. Permanently. Put me on the schedule.

I wasn't crazy about the idea of going back to White Castle, college degree in hand, but what else was I going to do? I was still interviewing for quote-unquote real jobs, when I wasn't flipping burgers, but I needed to make a few dollars (quite literally a few dollars) in the meantime.

I was back living at home with my parents for the time being, and it wasn't clear to me how much food they would be keeping in the refrigerator. My parents are both smaller than average people, and I'm much, much larger than the average person. If you ever look at a picture of my family, it looks like a man and his wife, their eight year-old son, and some random NFL linebacker. (My little brother is a year younger than I am.)

There was a lot of tension having to do with the fact that I'd yet to find a quote-unquote real job. Some people are able to nail one down before they graduate. If you can't, it's more or less guaranteed that you won't be able to, ever. You end up stuck interviewing for shit you find in the newspaper and on the Internets, which is all scams. Insurance, foreign construction, multilevel marketing and what have you. You'd think I would have been at an advantage, having gone to job fairs during both of my senior years at EBSU, but no.

The week after I graduated, I ran into a guy I went to high school with at a barbecue restaurant. Of course he was there working. He said he was thinking about moving into a shitty townhouse, in a complex filled with rednecks and Indian people, but he needed one more roommate in order to put together the $800/month rent. I could live there for $267/month. It was him and another guy, who worked at another barbecue restaurant. No, really.

And so I only lived at home for about 10 days after I graduated from college. I didn't even have to re-pack most of my shit. I just tossed it in the back of my car and drove up the street to my new, madd humble abode. I barely had enough money to live there, and I was probably less focused on my so-called job search living there than I would have been living at home with my parents, but at least I didn't have to sweat their constant bitching at me.

"Didn't I tell you to take out the trash six hours ago? That's why you can't find a job."

Fuck that noise, Jack.

All of a sudden I was that much more reliant on my income from White Castle. If you worked there full time, and you made what I made, i.e. peanuts, maybe you could have taken home $800/month. But they only ever let one or two people work there full-time. Whatever was the least they were required to by law. It was cheaper to keep a shedload of part-timers around, because you didn't have to pay them as much in benefits.

I was barely making ends meet. I was bringing home, on average, about $600/month, and I was paying upwards of half that in rent. (Personal finance experts don't recommend spending any more than about a third of your monthly take-home on rent.) That left me without about $300. Which seems like a lot of money, if you don't want to do anything with your life other than drink light beer anyway, but as revealed on one of the early episodes of the Cosby Show, when Theo was thinking about dropping out of high school, the working man never has as much money as he thinks he has.

Fortunately, I was working at White Castle. White Castle is one of the few fast food restaurants where they let you eat for free. Some places just let you order from the menu half off—and even then only when you're working that day. It says in Anthony Bourdain's excellent Kitchen Confidential that if you work in a fancy restaurant they feed you a staff meal, but it's not the fancy shit on the menu. It's baked chicken legs and noodle salad, or something along those lines. Like my childhood all over again.

*shudders at the thought*

And so hardly a day went by when I worked at White Castle that I didn't eat there. Literally. Even the first day, when I was just filling out forms and dropping off my Hep B immunization papers from the free clinic. Which I've done like four times, by the way, because I've worked in a lot of restaurants, and most of them I can't go back to. I'm so immune to hepatitis, I'm actually very susceptible. That's why I can't get with just any ol' woman. Well, I probably shouldn't. But I digress.

But it wasn't until I was out in the real world that I started really going to town on some White Castle. There was no limit to the amount of food they let you eat for free. All you had to do was ring it up and submit a receipt. I'm thinking either it cost them next to nothing at all, because it wasn't real food, or they somehow got a break on their taxes based on how many employee meals they serve, similar to how some companies get a tax break for employing special people. Maybe both.

I remember watching hoodrats eat three meals a day every day that they worked (before clocking in, at lunch and then again before they went home), back when I was in college, and shaking my head. But there I was, right there along with them. I had it worked out to where I was eating $18 a day worth of White Castle. My biggest meal was during my lunch break, and my smallest was before I went home. Just whatever I could stand to eat before I stumbled out of there. I experimented with different amounts before I found the perfect combination.

$18 worth of White Castle might seem like a lot, given what you pay for one of those tiny hamburgers. If one was $.50 (I never paid attention to what they cost), that would be over 30 hamburgers per day. That's a lot of

White Castle, though not an impossible amount. But the price of a meal at White Castle jumps way up, once you start adding in deep fried items and side dishes: onion rings, chicken rings, fish sandwiches and what have you. I never bothered with that shit before, because who has the money? I think they only put that shit on the menu for drunk yuppies on their way home from the club. But if the price is all the same to you, you might as well experiment, just to switch things up.

Plus, you can only eat so many of those hamburgers before your body starts talking back to you. I think it's the onions. They come dehydrated in a big 400 lb ostensibly bug-proof box. Just add water. I think dehydrating them and then rehydrating them makes them way stronger, like how beef jerky has a much more intense flavor than regular beef (which I find to be delicious on its own). They were always rumored to be cabbage that's flavored to taste like onion, rather than actual onions, but I can neither confirm nor deny that. I wasn't sworn to a vow of secrecy or anything, I'm just not sure how you would go about determining that. It does say onions on the box.

One thing I *can* tell you is that the chocolate shake is the exact same thing as a Frosty from Wendy's. I know... mind blowing, right? The box of chocolate milk-looking shake mix they pour into a machine to make it even says Wendy's on it. I'm not sure if they buy it from Wendy's, or if they buy it from the same place Wendy's buys their shake mix from. The latter seems more likely to me, based on my "business education."

One other thing: The cardboard bucket they use at KFC was invented by Dave Thomas from Wendy's. He used to own a shedload of KFC franchises. He sold them all to start Wendy's in the early '70s. (I didn't learn this in business school. I probably heard about it on the Food Network.)

Okay, I lied. I just thought of one more thing: Church's chicken is owned by Popeye's. And the part about it making black men sterile is kinda true, but not because the Klan put salt peter in it. Because it makes you fatter than a motherfucker. Even if you *could* get it up, it's gonna be that much more difficult to find a woman to have sex with.

Now, where was I? White Castle?

## 5 BAN KANYE WEST FROM THE GRAMMYS

So what I would do is I would bring in these magazines to read on my lunch break, while I was stuffing my face, and if I saw something interesting, I might write about it on my blog, when I got off.

These were magazines that had accumulated at my parents' house while I was in college. Mostly Rolling Stone and VIBE My mom put them in big boxes and made me take them with me when I moved out, even though there was a lot more room in their house than in that townhouse. I separated them into boxes by type and set all of the VIBE out by the curb, because VIBE magazine is only suitable for lames and flames.

It was in the break room of White Castle, bowels stuffed with radioactive onion dusted cabbage, a GI incident waiting to happen, that I read an article in Rolling Stone about Kanye West. I think it was the same one where he went to buy a necklace with a white (meaning pink) plastic Jesus medallion, a diamond encrusted bloody crown of thorns around its head, someone pointed out that it was white, and he took it back to the dealer's and demanded a black one, but don't quote me on that. This was over eight years ago.

Kanye was already on my list of things to do today (nullus), because I'd reviewed his album a few months before, not too long before I graduated from college, and I didn't really care for it. Of course I didn't care for the rapping on it, but I didn't care for the production, either.

There was a time when I did think he was a pretty good producer. His technique, so to speak, didn't involve anything other than taking old R&B records from the '70s, isolating a section of it, recording it onto some sort of digital sampler or computer, and speeding it up to the point where the vocals sounded like Alvin and the Chipmunks. His drums were ripped straight from old Pete Rock records, without so much as slightly altering them so as to throw off the scent.

But hey, rap music production is not rocket science. Some of the best rap songs of all time were made from simply looping up an old James Brown record.

I guess that wasn't enough for Kanye. The College Dropout is loaded down with gospel choirs, inbred kid from Deliverance-style violin, people singing through vocoders, additional keyboards on top of the keyboards already present in the sample, as if that's at all necessary… So many different elements in the mix. It's like late '80s-era Public Enemy, except it's not any good.

Then there's the fact that he's rapping on it, kicking lines like, "The way Kathie Lee needs Regis, that's the way I need Jesus," to use but one example of the many, many shitty lines on that album, because that's one of the few I have memorized. Why would I want to hear that? I wouldn't even want to hear a good song about Jesus. ("Jesus, etc." is not about Jesus, is it?)

It seemed like his ego was getting out of control. He should have been holed up in a studio somewhere coming up with new ways to rip off the RZA, letting people who know how to rap do the rapping.

His mom, who was quoted in the article, shed some light on how Kanye grew to be such an a-hole. She said that when he was a kid, she would encourage him to think that he was better than everyone else. This was the exact opposite of what my mom would tell me when I was a kid.

It became clear to me what was going on here. There was a flaw in Kanye's upbringing. His father, like so many black fathers, skipped town early on, and there wasn't a man around on a consistent basis to try to talk some sense into him. His mom would spoil him, feed into his worst impulses, and make him wear ridiculous outfits.

We all had that one kid in the neighborhood when we were growing up. The kid whose shoes were a little bit *too* clean. The kid who had socks in colors other than white (and maybe gray). Or black, if he was going to church or something. The kid with the cape and the t-shirt with a picture of his own face on it.

He wasn't even necessarily gay, he was just misguided.

I went home that afternoon and wrote a post called "Let's hunt and kill Kanye West's mother." It laid out the case against her, that she was the one ultimately responsible for Kanye's deeply flawed personality, and therefore she was ruining hip-hop, and it suggested that she be done away with.

Jokingly, of course. The title was of course a reference to the bit about Billy Ray Cyrus on Bill Hicks' Rant in E Minor, the best comedy album of all time, of ALL TIME, regardless of what SPIN magazine says (that's not a comedy magazine anyway), the fact that it's only intermittently funny notwithstanding. That's beside the point.

Kanye Doesn't Write His Own Lyrics

I can't say I was surprised to find out that Kanye doesn't write his own lyrics. I mean, they suck, so it's surprising that he would pay someone to write something that isn't any good, but besides that, no. I'm not surprised.

Maybe he instructs his ghostwriters to write bad lyrics on purpose, so it'll seem like he wrote them. Maybe his ghostwriters just aren't very good. If they were that good, they'd have successful careers of their own and wouldn't need a deal with G.O.O.D. Music.

I was informed, via the comments section of my blog, that "Jesus Walks" is essentially a cover version of a song by Rhymefest. A guy from Indianapolis, where Rhymefest is from, heard it on a mixtape. He lived across the street from a woman working as an escort out of her house. He thought about acquiring her services, so to speak, because of course it would have been convenient for him, and she wasn't bad-looking for a girl her age, but he worried that it would be weird with her being right there across the street.

On the one hand, you don't want someone like that to know where you live, because they might try to steal from you. But on the other hand, who knows. If you pay for it once or twice, she might hit you off with a "freebie." If you get one for free every now and again, each one that you pay for costs that much less, on average. It's the same concept behind the punch card system at Subway.

After I raised the issue on my blog (the songwriting, not the hoo-er), someone sent in an mp3. Yep, the Kanye song is really just a Rhymefest song. All Kanye did was erase Rhymefest's vocals and replace them with his own vocals. His verse is the exact same as Rhymefest's verse, except he says his own name in places where Rhymefest said his name. (Rappers love mentioning their own names.) Kanye West conveniently rhymes with Rhymefest, or who knows what he would have done.

And then Kanye did add a verse of his own. Er, a verse that wasn't there in the original. It's the verse with the line about Kathie Lee and Regis, natch. If you listen closely (or even not that closely), you'll notice that the first verse is in a way different style than the second verse. Kanye wasn't just switching up styles to show you how many styles he has. Kanye doesn't have style #1.

The fact that it's a song about how much he loves Jesus made the fact that he didn't really write it seem all the more ridonkulous. I mean, I could see if it was a song about how much you enjoy throwing money in women's faces, Don Draper-style. Theoretically, if you believe what it says in the Bible, wouldn't Jesus know that your song about him was a scam?

I suggested that "Jesus Walks" shouldn't be allowed to win a Grammy. Even if it was in fact a song about making it rain on these hoes, I don't think it should have been allowed to win a Grammy, because it's a rap song, and in rap music it's assumed that the guy singing the song is the guy who wrote the song. It's a singer-songwriter form. Giving a Grammy to a rap song that's ghostwritten would be the equivalent of giving a Grammy to a singer who lip synchs.

The thing is, the Grammys did give an award to a singer who lip synched. Well, they've probably given a lot of awards to singers who lip synch live, but they gave an award to Milli Vanilli, who didn't even sing on their actual album. It wasn't even two people singing on that Milli Vanilli album. It was three, and one of them was a woman. Tha fuck?

A lot of people forget that once it was revealed that Milli Vanilli couldn't really sing, the Grammys didn't ask for those statues back. Milli Vanilli gave those statues back of their own volition. The Grammys apparently weren't concerned with maintaining their credibility.

I should have realized there was no point in trying to talk any sense into them.

But I did. I created a petition, using one of those sites where you can create a petition for free in exchange for the page being plastered with banner ads that would probably ruin your computer if you clicked on them. Some of them are so tempting, because they have a monkey you have to hit over the head with a club, whack-a-mole-style. You can tell they're a scam, because they don't even advertise a product. But they look so easy! I almost clicked on one of them back in the late '90s. I followed it around some with my mouse, but following it around with your mouse doesn't do anything to your computer.

In order to promote the petition, I sent out a press release using one of those sites where you can send out a free press release, and then for an additional $25 they'll send it to a real email address. The way it works is, you enter in your information, write a press release, press submit and send it out, and then a guy from the company calls you using the number you just gave them and tries to upsell you on the $25 premium version.

$25 was a lot of money for me at the time, but I figured what the fuck. If it worked, it would be worth it. Imagine if you sent out a press release about how an organization whose name you just pulled out of your ass is collecting signatures to have Kanye West banned from the Grammys, and someone actually mentioned it on the news. This had the potential to be one of the very best things I've done in my career, so to speak.

The information from my press release was in fact mentioned on the news, but I don't know if the press release company had anything to do with it. That was probably just another scam I fell victim to. It seems like I got more traction out of just emailing it to people. Some of the more credible hip-hop sites, to the extent that there could be a credible hip-hop site, fronted on me, but some of the more obscure hip-hop sites ran with it, and it gradually trickled upwards from there, thus defying both Reaganomics and basic laws of physics.

The highest profile media organization to report on it was one of those drive-time radio programs for older black people. I want to say it was the Tom Joyner Morning Show, but I think there's like four of them and they're all interchangeable in my mind. I know Steve Harvey has one. He might have the top one of them all. He's big time now. He wrote that self help book for lonely black women, which I heard was an absolute joke, and not only was it turned into a movie, but people actually saw it. Amazing. Those shows hold a lot of sway in the black community. Which makes the fact that they'll apparently report pretty much anything as news all the more disturbing.

Several people hit me up saying they heard about my petition on the radio. I felt a sense of accomplishment. It helped to justify, at least on an emotional level, getting duped out of $25, which I was really starting to miss. I *still* miss that $25.

Other ideas I had to promote the petition weren't the best ideas in the world. I started a separate site, devoted solely to trying to get Kanye West banned from the Grammys, and it never received as much traffic as my own site. So not as many people saw it, and not as many people got a chance to sign the petition. As Robert DeNiro would say, it defeated its own purpose. But I did come up with a few amusing posts. And a few people contributed amusing posts of their own.

Time went by and I gradually lost interest, to the point where it was getting close to the Grammys and I had yet to submit the petition to the Recording Academy, or whoever you would submit a petition like that to. I clicked around on the Grammys website, and I think I did find an email address and send someone a link to the page with the petition. Of course they never emailed me back. That address probably just goes to the guy who designed the page. I should have researched, found out who's really in charge, and tried to find a phone number or something. Is it one of the guys from

Toto?

The night of the Grammys, I was working the evening shift at a K-Mart. I couldn't afford to take off. My financial situation was all fucked the fuck up. In just the time since I'd been out of school, i.e. less than a year, I had quit White Castle, spent a few months working at one of my roommates' barbecue restaurants, quit working there, gone back to White Castle for a few more months and finally walked off the job mid shift, Half Baked-style. I'd work and quit a few more minimum wage jobs before it occurred to me that eventually it would get to the point where I wouldn't even be able to get a minimum wage job. Then what would I do? I found a job I could just barely stand, and I've been there ever since.

Kanye did end up winning a Grammy for "Jesus Walks." Rhymefest, who's listed in the credits as a co-writer on the song, also received a statue, though I'm not sure what difference it makes. Would it have made a difference if the middle aged gospel singers who sang "Girl You Know It's True" received statues along with the guys from Milli Vanilli? I stand by the point I was trying to make in having Kanye West banned from the Grammys.

A few weeks later, Kanye West came to St. Louis. I stopped by my parents' house, and my old man pointed out to me where it said in the paper that Kanye West would be performing in St. Louis that night, and they wondered if I would be there. The actual newspaper, mind you. Not some bullshit alt-weekly.

I thought about going down there, but of course I didn't have any money for a ticket. I couldn't just show the guy working the door where it said in the paper that people were expecting me to be there. People here in St. Louis aren't very media savvy. And who knows, they may have been under strict orders from Kanye not to let me in, if I did show up. I even thought about hanging out on the street outside the stadium where he was performing.

Homeless people sleep on the sidewalk next to the building during the summer, because it's air conditioned. They air condition the outdoors directly adjacent to the building, for some reason. It must be a union thing. One time, on the way to see Bruce Springsteen, I saw a homeless guy who had a big glass jar that he was using as a restroom, like the homeless guy from In Living Color. He wasn't using it that very moment, thank God. He just had it sitting there next to him. "Born in the USA" started playing in my head.

# 6 DON'T HATE FREE SPEECH, HATE YOURSELF

I lived in that townhouse for about a year, and then I moved into an apartment in a rundown four family flat, where I had just one roommate. I was paying about the same as I was paying to live in that townhouse, which was good, because it's not like I was making any more money.

There weren't as many Indian people in the area, but it just so happens that the other unit on the first floor (where we lived) was occupied by Indian people. They seemed to always be cooking smelly Indian food. Go figure.

My employment situation was more erratic than ever. At one point, I was making as much as $800/month. I was living high on the hog, going to the grocery store and not worrying about if I had enough money to put on a drunk. I was still eating a lot of bologna on white bread, but I didn't give a shit.

I will admit, I miss working at White Castle for the free meals. I've been working in retail for about seven years now, if you can imagine, and I think that's been a bad move. I should have stayed working in fast food, if only for the free or discounted meals. Not just because I enjoy fast food, which I do, but because if you eat for free or half off, it's like you're getting paid that much more.

That's one piece of advice I have for today's youth: If you can't get a job making any more than $8/hour, which you probably can't, pick fast food over retail. In addition to the money you save on food, the people you work with are better people (if not actually good), and the customers are *way* better people.

Reasonable people only go to the store occasionally, when they actually need something. People who shop for recreational purposes are horrible, horrible people—much worse in terms of character than black guys in prison, but not as dangerous, because they're women.

Adjusting to life as a minimum wage employee, and the fact that I couldn't do anything else, was difficult, which had an effect on my behavior and so I was in and out of a job a lot that year. I was averaging one new job every three months. Some places I would walk off mid-shift, some places I would just stop showing up. Sometimes I'd just pretend I found another job, and then I had to try to find something before I ran out of money.

I spent the summer of 2005 just kinda sitting around in my underwear listening to music. It was one of the very best times of my life. I had saved upwards of $1,000 from the last place where I worked, and I figured fuck it, I could afford to take a couple of months off, like a school teacher.

I had to be very careful with my money. The key is not to do a whole lot other than sit around. You can't go anywhere in your car without burning gasoline, and if you go anywhere on foot that's just gonna make you hungry. You'll end up spending that much more money on food. I wasn't even drinking as much as I used to.

I had this big box fan that I'd set in the doorway, and I had a few great albums that came out around that time that I'd turn way up to drown out the sound of the box fan. Cold Roses by Ryan Adams & The Cardinals, Separation Sunday by the Hold Steady, and Twin Cinema by the New Pornographers remain some of my favorite albums of all time to this day, and not just because I've heard them all literally a million times. They really are the best albums of all time.

One day I got an email from a guy from the Riverfront Times, the local equivalent of the Village Voice, here in St. Louis. This was before it was owned by the Village Voice. Or rather, before the Village Voice was purchased by the chain of alt-weeklies that owned the Riverfront Times and changed its name to Village Voice Media. But not too long. A mere matter of weeks, as I recall.

My blog had been featured in the RFT once or twice before. One time I can recall is when I wrote an article speaking out against public breastfeeding, which I find to be mostly an excuse for exhibitionism. You never see a woman with a really nice body breastfeeding in public. She might get attacked. It's always the last woman in the world you'd want to see topless.

You see the same principle at work in the HBO series Girls. Girls star and creator Lena Dunham, who has the most hideous body a woman could possibly have at the age of 25 (somehow much worse than significantly larger women) gets naked at least once per episode, but it took me until about four episodes in to realize that none of the other girls would be stripping down. They weren't even taking off their clothes during sex scenes.

She's not making any artistic statement, she's just antagonizing men.

In addition to being featured in the Riverfront Times, my post on public breastfeeding led to what must have been one of the very first beefs between a blogger and a podcaster. I could be mistaken, but I think podcasting was only invented circa 2005.

My post was discussed on an episode of a podcast called Soccer Girl. Soccer Girl would post pictures of herself naked, taking a bath and what have you, to try to generate interest in her show. I went to listen to the show where she was talking about me, saw those pictures, and it was clear to me why she took offense.

If I had two more hands, I would give those cans four thumbs down. They looked like the white equivalent of Janet Jackson's cans when she had that wardrobe malfunction at the Super Bowl, only less voluminous. And this girl wasn't nearly as old.

Ben Westhoff from the Riverfront Times wanted to interview me for an article in the paper's music section. We agreed to meet at this Mexican place not too far from where I was living at the time. It was a sort of no name brand version of a Q'doba or a Chipotle, before there was such a thing as

Q'doba or Chipotle.

(Note: I'm sure both Q'doba and Chipotle have been around for like a million years, but they haven't been around here for very long. It takes a while for things to get here to St. Louis—if they get here at all.)

This first interview was cut short both by Westhoff's GI issues and the fact that I'm not a very good interview. He needed to get up and go stand somewhere where there wasn't anyone within earshot, and we weren't getting anywhere anyway. I'm not the best in the world at answering questions, and the truth of the matter is that I don't have a very interesting story. I'm just a guy who has a blog.

There was a second, similarly unproductive interview that took place at a restaurant that's since been closed due to an unfortunate demographic shift in the Delmar Loop, where it's located.

They built this light rail system between downtown and the airport. It also goes to the ghetto and to a mall. If they just got rid of the part where it goes to the ghetto, it would be fine, if not particularly useful to people who could actually use public transportation. Kids were taking the train to the mall to beat each other up and steal. The mall was able to solve that problem, via profiling. So the kids just started going to the Loop.

The Loop is hamstrung in dealing with this issue, compared to the mall, because it's not a mall, it's a street. You can't just kick people out of the outdoors. That would violate Newton's laws of physics. You can make them go one block over, which is in the city, at a certain hour, if they're underage, but it's not like they can't still shoot each other one block over. The city could care less, because they have a different philosophy when it comes to law enforcement. They try not to be there when a crime takes place. It's always a surprise to them when something bad happens in the exact same place where something bad always happens.

The part of the Loop that's in the city has been rechristened Barack Obama Blvd, because there's a pizza place there that the president declared his favorite, so as to not have to pick a restaurant in Chicago and probably piss off half the city. There's an actual street sign that sits right out in front of a Church's chicken. You can see it in the background of a recent news report about a driveby shooting, in which you can also see a half-naked (at best) hoodrat running for cover. Local TV news was on the scene to report on another disturbance, earlier that evening, when shots rang out.

Streets named after Barack Obama seem destined to become the new streets named after Martin Luther King, Jr., in that they're the last place you want to be if you're at all concerned with your personal safety. St. Louis can't claim credit for much, but we can take credit for having one of the first, if not the very first of them. We also have one of the first elementary schools named after the president. It's in a school district right out of the movie Lean on Me. My little brother used to work there. One time he took my Nintendo Wii to work for the kids to play with (no Boutros) and one of them stole it.

After that second interview, I was informed that I couldn't have any more free lunch courtesy of the RFT expense account. (Of course I wasn't paying for these lunches.) They must have been under the impression that I was trying to string this process along, to try to get as much free food as possible. The RFT is not the New York Times. And this was back before running ads for white slavery had become an existential concern for the alt-weekly.

Back in the mid '00s, Craigslist was still the place to go to find a date for the evening that costs money (but is guaranteed to end well). Unlike classified ads in newspapers, they'd often include a photo of your date, so you had an idea of what you were getting, if not the most accurate idea. As revealed in the great film Risky Business, if you try to cop a hooker from a newspaper, you could end up with a guy.

Risky business indeed.

Craigslist had to stop running ads for hookers, er, adult services, because serial killers were hiring girls from Craigslist and then hacking them up. They probably weren't even paying them first. Not that it matters. Craigslist was under a lot of pressure from Congress to put the kibosh on that. Even though Craigslist is free to use, it probably still makes a shedload of money.

Enter Backpage.com. Nullus. It may have existed before Craigslist had to get rid of its adult services department, but it only took off once Craigslist had to get rid of its adult services department. It's now the place to go to find a date for the evening that costs money (but is guaranteed to end well).

This coincided with a time in which alt-weeklies can't make as much money from ads for local restaurants, apartment rentals, herpes medicine, strip club fliers and what have you, because who's got the money to go out these days? From what I understand, if the Village Voice was forced to stop running ads for white slavery on Backpage.com, it might have to go out of business.

Week in and week out, as I write this, the New York Times is running op-eds about how pimps are using Backpage.com to advertise the wares of middle school-age girls, as if that's the only age of girl you can rent from Backpage.com. It's obvious to me that this is just a roundabout way to drive a competitor out of business. The New York Times smells blood in the water.

I'm officially Team Village Voice, and not because I condone the buying and selling of 13 year-old girls. They need to cut that shit out. And the thing is, they have. They don't allow you to advertise anyone who's clearly underage, and they've been fully cooperative with law enforcement. A lot of these facts about the prevalence of white slavery in this country are obviously made up. Who are you going to believe, the Village Voice or Ashton Kutcher?

Don't let me find out Ashton Kutcher has stock in the New York Times. I've heard he has stock in a lot of companies. He gets magazines to let him write articles in which he shills for companies he owns stock in without giving full disclosure.

And I don't buy for a minute that Ashton Kutcher wasn't aware that Jerry Sandusky was making love to kids from behind, when he jumped to the defense of Joe Paterno on Twitter, when Paterno was fired from Penn State. Even though I kinda agreed with Ashton Kutcher on that one.

If you look at the facts of the case, regardless of whether not JoePa called the cops on Jerry Sandusky or did anything to try to prevent the guy from making love to any more kids from behind, which he didn't, he did in fact report it to his superiors. Which is all you're allowed to do anywhere I ever worked. You can't just call the cops. You have to call your manager, and your manager calls the cops, in case you call the wrong number.

If he didn't already die of a heart attack, I'd encourage Joe Paterno to try to get his job back.

I got another email from Ben Westhoff. He wanted to stop by the apartment and observe me in my natural element, like a polar bear at the zoo. He wanted to see how the sausage is made and the fudge is packed, so to speak. No homo.

I thought maybe the RFT wasn't gonna bother running an article on me, but come to find out my article got bumped up from the music section to a full-on feature. That's one of the few perks of living in a city like St. Louis: if you do anything at all interesting, they'll put you on the front page of the paper, as if it's actual news.

I think what sealed it was when Westhoff emailed me to see if I had anything I could send him that would make for good fodder for a feature, and I forwarded him a buncha emails I received from people upset about my campaign to have Kanye West disqualified from the Grammys. This was coming up on a year since the beginning of the campaign and several months since the actual ceremony.

Kanye's childhood babysitter and many of his relatives from Chicago all chimed in. Even his mom apparently Googled her own name and found the post in which I suggested that she should be done away with. (Jokingly, of course.) I didn't confirm that it really was her at the time, and obviously I can't now. She died a few years later in a tragic plastic surgery accident.

After the article ran in the paper, a guy named Clyde Smith tried to call the RFT's sterling journalistic reputation into question, because they didn't have any way of proving that that was really Kanye West's mother, as if the article hinged on it really being Kanye West's mother. It could have been someone pretending to be Kanye West's mother, and it wouldn't have made a difference. (But it wasn't, as far as I know.)

The year before, while I was trying to have Kanye West disqualified from the Grammys, Clyde Smith tried to have me disqualified from... I don't know, appearing on the Internets? Because of my frequent use of the term no homo. He suggested that no other blogs should link to my blog. If no other blogs link to your blog, your blog doesn't rank as highly in Google, which is no good for traffic.

The only person who bit was a guy named Oliver Wang, an ethnic studies professor and political correctness advocate who also spoke out against the use of the term. I called him on it, and he claimed it didn't have anything to do with Clyde Smith; he was just tidying up his blogroll. Nullus. I was actually more concerned with the fact that he's a liar than I was with whether or not he linked to my blog. And that's why I posted his phone number on my blog and told people it was Ashlee Simpson's phone number.

I was watching her show on MTV, a spinoff of Jessica Simpson's Newlyweds. This was back before Ashlee Simpson got her nose fixed. It was truly bizarre-looking but I'm not gonna lie—I kinda liked it. Sometimes I like girls with weird noses. Someone wrote in with a phone number that they said was hers. I put it up on my blog in a post called "Call Ashlee Simpson yourself and tell her how ugly you think she is," or something to that effect.

A few weeks go by, and then there was the incident on SNL. Ashlee Simpson was trying to lip synch, Milli Vanilli-style, and something must have happened to the tape. Milli Vanilli got caught the same way. SNL is of course live, hence the name, so everyone saw it and knew she was lip synching. It was a huge scandal. Perhaps you remember.

One of the guys from her band, desperate to protect his indie rock cred, went on the Internets and posted her phone number, in retaliation. It may have been on MySpace, if MySpace was around at the time. I can't recall. I don't think it was up for very long before Ashlee Simpson was able to have it removed. But not before the media picked up on it.

Dumbass kids saw reports on Ashlee Simpson's phone number being posted on the Internets and went on Google looking for "Ashlee Simpson's phone number" or "call Ashlee Simpson," and one of the main things they found was my post with what was supposedly Ashlee Simpson's phone number. Whoever's phone number that was apparently got inundated with calls. They wrote in to say that they weren't Ashlee Simpson. Once again I had been duped.

I took the part with the phone number down but left the rest of the post there. But then it occurred to me that I could just replace the phone number with someone else's phone number, and that person would be inundated with calls. And the rest, as they say, is history.

# 7 THAT WASN'T NOT FUNNY

Ben Westhoff wanted to know what time he should come by to watch the master at work, so to speak. I told him it didn't matter. He must have been under the impression that this was an actual job. Typically, I'll roll out of bed whenever I happen to be done sleeping, check the news, and it I see something that interests me I'll write about it. Some days I wouldn't write anything at all. It's not like I had a boss, or a salary.

For the purposes of this experiment, I put on a pair of pants and relocated my base of operations from my bedroom to the apartment's living room. I wasn't about to have another guy sitting there in my bedroom while I work. I'm not big on the idea of guys in my bedroom, period. Even girls, unless they're there to get busy. And obviously I wasn't about to hang out with another guy in my underwear.

There was a while between when I woke up and when Westhoff showed up to the apartment, so I ended up checking the news, and either I wrote about all there was to write about that day before he got there, or there wasn't anything to write about that day. Damn. He wouldn't be able to watch me work. Instead, I just kinda walked him through what I usually do. Which of course turned out to be useless for the purpose of writing the article.

If I would have been thinking, I would have picked a fight with someone the day before. That way he could have watched me slander someone in real time. It would have been exciting. Sometimes I used to pace the floor of the apartment when I couldn't come up with anything. Sometimes I used to start drinking way early just to see what I could come up with.

Westhoff wanted something to drink, and I of course didn't keep anything in the apartment except beer and my roommate's Gatorade. He asked me if there was a soda machine nearby, and I told him I thought there was one at the laundromat on the corner.

I was having to take my laundry to the laundromat down the street, because one of the neighbors caught me using her machine and put up a note saying I wasn't allowed to use her machine. Some kind of neighbor she was! One time I did a load and forgot it was down there for a while. I think that's how she figured out it was me. (My pants are madd big.) I had to be more careful about using her machine. Eventually, she ratted me out to the landlord.

There was that Gatorade in the fridge, but not only was it not mine, it had become somewhat of a contentious topic. My roommate had started keeping a bottle of Gatorade in the fridge at all times, after an incident in which he was given the nickname Rainbow. You know... from the symbol for gay people.

He had gone to this party, and it ended up being one of those parties where very expensive party favors are handed out, if you catch my drift. The next morning, he coughed up a little bit of blood, and he demanded to be driven to the hospital. He couldn't just drive himself, because his car wasn't there, and he wouldn't listen to reason, that coughing up a little bit of blood the next day is a natural consequence of going H.A.M. like that.

At the hospital, the doctor took one look at him, gave him a bottle of Gatorade and sent him on his merry little way. He's been known as Rainbow ever since. But only if you want to run the risk of him swinging on you. He's Irish, and hence he's as prone to violence as he is drinking.

Later he got this dog, Eberhardt, named after one of the founders of Anheuser Busch, and people would joke was that it was gay, as well. It was a decent-sized dog, and it was very handsome, as far as dogs go (no Boutros), but it didn't seem to have a whole lot of scrap in it. It seemed to be intimidated by other dogs half its size, and it would whimper when you'd yell at it. Or so I've been told.

Eberhardt was a pure-bred boxer. Supposedly, my roommate got a very good deal on him from a guy who was a breeder. You know how it is when people supposedly get a good deal on a dog from a breeder. Best case scenario, it doesn't drop dead all of sudden two weeks later. If it was really worth $1,000, why would they sell it to you for $40?

My roommate didn't want to get the dog neutered, because he thought one day he might be able to rent it out to stud, as a source of ancillary income, so sometimes it would get excited and try to rape inanimate objects. One time it tried to rape the corner of the couch I was sitting on. I was sitting dangerously close to that corner.

One time, my roommate's girlfriend brought her dog over and we were all watching an episode of Entourage. The dogs were sitting on a rug by the front door, where Eberhardt would often sleep. They didn't have any interest in the show. At one point, I looked over, and Eberhardt was licking the other dog's genitalia. The other dog was also male. I pointed this out to my roommate, and he took his shoe off and threw it at them, to bust up the proceedings.

After that time it raped the corner of the couch I was sitting on, I went on the Internets and jokingly threatened to kill it, referring to the infamous gay panic defense used by the two rednecks who killed Matthew Shepard. The defense didn't work in that case, but I figured a court might be more lenient if it was just a dog. Plus, it was a joke anyway, so what difference did it make?

A guy from a gay newspaper called the NY Blade must have Googled Kanye West and saw the post in which I jokingly threatened to kill my roommate's gay dog. He was working on an article on Kanye, who had just taken a bold and courageous stance against homophobia, in an MTV special in which he also showed off several paintings he had made as a teenager. It was a weird show. I didn't know what the fuck was going on. I thought maybe he was about to come out of the closet.

Maybe this was just a half-step, to test the water. Gay people who are thinking about coming out of the closet will sometimes start out by doing something kinda gay, to gauge their friends and families' reactions. They might wear a gay outfit, or compliment another guy's looks. Martin Lawrence has a bit about this in his great standup comedy film You So Crazy. Remember when we used to go down to the creek?

A friend of mine in high school's father lived two doors down from a guy who famously got fired from his job for randomly showing up to work one day in a dress. There was a big article about it in the RFT back in the day. My friend's father said that before this guy up and started wearing a dress there were signs. He would show up to fishing trips wearing those extra-tight coach's shorts a size too small, to accentuate the bulge in his crotch.

Kanye was held up in this article in the gay newspaper as a paragon of progressive values in the hip-hop community, while I was cited as an example of the rampant homophobia. I'm not homophobic at all, I just find some gay jokes funny. I'm so accepting of gay people (nullus) that I don't have a problem telling a joke that they might find offensive.

The NY Blade has long since gone out of business. It was one of the first newspapers to die off when the economy shit the bed and print media took it especially hard, because who needs print media. Because it obviously lacked credibility.

On the way down the street to the Laundromat to get that soda, I was informed that we could get into several local strip clubs for free. Westhoff asked me if I'd be interested. I'm not sure what kind of guy he takes me as.

He had written an article about the local mob boss who owns a few of the strip clubs around here and his effort to get out the vote in the '04 presidential election. He was giving people a ride to the polls, because he must have been afraid that Bush would try to outlaw strip clubs if he got reelected. I know Attorney General John Ashcroft (who's from here in Missouri) was trying to crack down on pr0n.

Or who knows, maybe he just felt it was his civic duty, as someone who had the means, to make sure everyone was able to have his voice heard. I don't want to cast aspersions on the guy, especially given the important service he provides. I remember Acorn or some group was also handing out menthol cigarettes to homeless people who agreed to vote in that election.

Westhoff had the rest of the afternoon off, and we didn't have anything else to do, so I suggested we take in an episode of Entourage. We had HBO On Demand in the apartment, despite my financial situation, because it's important to have priorities. Westhoff had that soda. It was a little early in the afternoon, but I decided to have a beer.

I put on Entourage, and all of sudden there was a scratching sound coming from the rear of the apartment. I had locked Eberhardt in the back bedroom, and it must have heard Entourage was on and got excited. It wanted out. Either it thought its master was home, or that song by Satellite Party, Perry Farrell's mid '00s-era substitute Jane's Addiction, brought out the freak in it, via sense memory

I told Westhoff that that was my roommate's dog, and it was best to leave it back there. It couldn't be trusted. He said he didn't have a problem with dogs, and it was alright if I let it out. I tried to tell him it was best if we just left it back there. He gave me a look similar to the look my third college roommate gave me when I told him I didn't bother to vote in the 2000 presidential election, despite the fact that I spent my every waking hour back in those days watching cable news. That look always bothered me.

So fine, I let the damn thing out.

It just so happens that Westhoff was sitting at the same corner of the couch that had fallen victim to rape. That corner of the couch was a survivor. I was sitting in a separate chair, because I'm not as comfortable sitting on a couch with another guy watching TV. It's not a sexual thing or anything. It's just, I don't find that to be necessary, if there's another chair in the room.

Eberhardt had that look, like either it needed to use the restroom or something bad was about to happen. It couldn't go outside, because the yard wasn't fenced in and it wasn't the kind of dog that had the sense to go outside, handle its business, and knock when it was ready to be let back in. I had a dog like that when I was a kid. It was smarter than most people. I think some of my intelligence rubbed off on it.

Eberhardt started nervously circling that corner of the couch that was a survivor. I knew what could potentially happen, but I didn't want to say anything, because I had already been made to look like a bad person for locking it in a back bedroom, like a special relative.

All of a sudden, it hopped up on its two hind legs, mounted Westhoff's leg, popped a full-on doggy boner and started going to town on Westhoff's leg. It was one of the most disgusting things I've ever seen (but not for the same-sex nature of the attack, mind you). I can only imagine how it felt. No Boutros. Having that dog-rod repeatedly rammed into your leg like that, trying to impregnate the crevice between your calf and your lower thigh region.

Westhoff, to his credit, didn't violently attack Eberhardt. Say this much about the man: He walks it like he talks it. He really doesn't have a problem with dogs.

We made plans to visit those free strip clubs, and Westhoff went home to take a Silkwood shower and do some serious soul-searching. Later that day, or maybe another day (I can't remember anymore), we would meet up to head over to the Eastside. All of the strip clubs here in St. Louis are across the river, in Illinois, a 30-45 minute drive from where I was living at the time. There's only a few strip clubs here in Missouri, and they're all special. Either you're not allowed to drink, or the girls have to wear pasties, or you're not allowed to touch them... Missouri is like the town in Footloose if it were an entire state.

Southern Illinois, on the other hand, is one big free for all. Westhoff explained this to me on the way over. He said that some of these towns in southern Illinois don't have laws per se. Later I checked Wikipedia, and it really does say that Sauget, Illinois, formerly known as Monsanto, Illinois, doesn't have laws. It might be different now, because there's a semi-professional baseball team that plays there. It used to be just a strip club, a concert venue for Juggalos and a Monsanto plant. The strippers' skin is especially firm because of the air pollution. You'll never get a lapdance quite like the one you get in Sauget.

We were almost killed by Willie Nelson on the way over. There's a concert venue that's sort of in between where I was living at the time and downtown. I drove past it on the way to the highway. The Eastside is like a half an hour drive straight east. As Willie Nelson's bus was hanging a left onto Delmar, going the same way I was going but not on the highway, I saw that there was a big-ass picture of Willie Nelson on the side of it. That's how I knew that it was Willie Nelson's tour bus. If I looked closely, maybe I would have seen clouds of smoke billowing from the doors and windows.

Fifteen or twenty minutes later, as we were nearing downtown St. Louis on the highway, I looked up and saw the same bus. Willie Nelson had somehow gotten ahead of me on the highway. He must have had better directions. I've been living in St. Louis my entire left, except for the five years I spent out in Chicken Switch, but I only venture into certain areas when I absolutely have to. I'm a true West County-ite.

I was driving faster than Willie Nelson, and I was embarrassed that he was beating me, so I tried to pass him on the right. As I did, he started to merge into the lane I was in and damn near crashed into me. I don't know if he was purposely trying to fuck with me, he wasn't paying attention to what he was doing, because he was high on weed, or he just couldn't see me, because I was trying to pass on the right, which you're not supposed to. At any rate, he almost killed me.

A collision with Willie Nelson's tour bus would be especially tragic, because it's run on leftover fryer grease from fast food restaurants. Imagine if you ran into it, it caught fire, you burned alive, and when the meat wagon got there all they could smell was weed and French fries. Like firefighters who can't eat bacon, which smells like burning human flesh (and tastes delicious), they'd never be able to eat French fries again.

So we got over to the Eastside. Westhoff explained to the guy at the door that we were down with the mafia, the guy at the door consulted with another guy, and we were in. I couldn't believe it. We looked like a bunch of broke college kids. I'd try it again today, but I shudder to think what would happen if the guy at the door realized I was full of shit. It's a known fact that they break people's legs for trying to reach inside of the dancers. They take you right out back.

I couldn't afford to get a lapdance or anything. I only had enough to buy a couple of drinks and toss a few dollars at the stage, as a show of appreciation, and even that I had to borrow from my mom. I actually had to go over to my parents' house and explain to her that I needed to "borrow" some money to go to a strip club, as part of a story about me that would be in the paper. It was like getting blood from a stone, but not because she was necessarily against me going to a strip club. She just likes to obstruct a process, for her own personal amusement.

When you only bring a certain amount of money to the club, you have to be conservative with your tipping. If the next girl onstage is not up to your usual high standards, it's important to get up and move to a table further from the stage, to make it clear that she doesn't have anything coming. Otherwise, you look like an a-hole. Some of those clubs on the Eastside are fully nude.

There was an incident where the token Asian stripper took to the stage for a three song hair metal cycle and my roommate and I had to switch tables. My roommate explained to Westhoff that he "didn't dine on Chinese." I don't either, generally speaking, but not as a rule or anything. It's just not what I prefer, if I only have a limited amount of money to spend. If I'd brought $100 with me for the evening, maybe I would have stuck around.

I tried explaining this to Westhoff, and he flashed me a look similar to the one he gave me when he found out that I had locked Eberhardt in a back bedroom. Then he tucked a few dollars into the Asian stripper's g-string.

# 8 BEST WEEK EVER

At the time, I joked that the week that I turned 25 years old was the very best week of my life, with the caveat that I hadn't had very many really good weeks up until that point. I haven't had very many really good weeks since, so it could be that it really was the very best week of my life. Let's take a look at the stats.

Things kicked off with my parents buying me not one, but two new pairs of shoes. At that point it had been a while since I had a new pair of shoes. I had been out of college for a couple of years, and I'd been either out of work or not working anywhere where I could easily afford to buy myself shoes. When you're 22 years old and you're thinking about the minimum amount of money you need to make in order to get by, you don't think about the fact that you're gonna have to buy your own shoes.

I went with my parents to this new, weird mall on the outskirts of a remote, unfortunate part of St. Louis. In order to get there you either have to take a bus or a car trip that's not on the way to anything else. We went there more so just to check it out. It had been built at some point when I was in college and none of us had been there. It wasn't my actual birthday, and I wasn't expecting to receive shoes for my birthday. Of course I would never ask for shoes for my birthday, even if I really needed them. I'm a guy.

The St. Louis Mills is neither a real mall with stores anyone ever heard of like the Gap and Footlocker, nor an outlet mall like they have in some of the tourist towns in Florida, with designer factory outlets, stores that sell remaindered hardcover copies of books no one wanted to read, so on and so forth. The best way I can think to describe it is if a Marshall's or a Ross for Less (which I believe is the West Coast equivalent of a Marshall's) was an entire mall. I would urge you to make sure that anything you buy from there isn't an "irreg," and if it is, that it isn't so fucked the fuck up that you couldn't possibly wear it. A little blood on your tie is one thing, but what are you going to do with a shirt that doesn't have holes for your arms? Cut your arms off?

We stopped by this store where you can get two pairs of shoes for the price of one. And by "price of one," I mean the price of one relatively inexpensive pair of shoes. None of this $150 for a pair of shoes that some gangbanger might rob you for bullshit. I think it was $50 all in. I got a pair of white and green "casual wear" shoes made by Mark Ecko, who makes hip-hop clothes for people who live in rural areas, and a pair of knockoff Air Jordans made by Vans. They were a knockoff version of one of the early Air Jordans, with the fake snakeskin around the toe and the air bubble beneath the heel, to make you jump higher.

I still have both of those pairs of shoes. The Eckos I wore quite a bit, and I would look like a bum if I continued to wear them at this point. I know this because I took a few pictures of them and posted them on my blog, which is the thing to do in a certain sad corner of the Internets, and people were giving me shit about them as if I couldn't afford a decent pair of shoes. Which was true, but still. Later, Dallas Penn bought me a pair of the kind of fancy Nikes they wear in New York. I believe they're called Dunks, but don't quote me on that. I still wear them to this day.

I never did wear those Vans much. At the time, I was keeping them until I wore out the Eckos, so I could possibly go half a decade or so without having to buy tennis shoes. But I don't wear tennis shoes much anyway, because of my work in retail, and I've got those Nikes, and when I started getting paid to blog for XXL I switched to a New Balance 993 as my main tennis shoe. At about $100 a pair, they'll run you, but you can wear them for about two years before they look at all worn, and it's not like you have to toss them out at that point. The pair I have now were maybe a couple of years old when I got let go from XXL, and that's been over a year ago.

Note that I was up on both Vans and wearing the same pair of shoes forever long before Lil B. He jacked my swag, as the kids these days say.

Later that week, I had something known as an Outlaw Burger from Jack in the Box. The Outlaw Burger is Jack in the Box's knockoff version of Burger King's Western Bacon Cheeseburger, from the 1990s, as immortalized on a skit from that first Tenacious D album. It has cheese, bacon, barbecue sauce and onion rings on it. I don't think it was new at that point, but it had been recently re-released, perhaps because it was coming up on spring, Jack in the Box knew people would have a taste for barbecue, and the Outlaw Burger has barbecue sauce on it.

One day I was driving past a Jack in the Box, and I saw a sign for it in the window. I just so happened to have five dollars or so in my pocket, and I said to myself, fuck it. I'm about to go get one of those Outlaw Burgers. Was it the best sandwich I ever ate? No, it was from Jack in the Box. But there is something oddly fulfilling about seeing an ad for fast food and then going to cop the thing you just saw an ad for. And this was at a time in my life when I didn't always have money for fast food. There's nothing worse than seeing an ad for fast food and not being able to afford it. It's like not being able to feed your children. I would imagine. But worse, because you're the one that's going hungry.

# 9 CAREER OPPORTUNITIES

That week, XXL magazine was in the process of revamping its website from a static page with an order form to sign up for a subscription to the dead tree version of the magazine, and a letter from the editor that they only bothered to update every now and again, to a full-on modern rap music magazine website, with daily features, blogs, audio, music videos, pictures of half-naked women, so on and so forth. I watched with keen interest, having run a hip-hop blog for a few years at that point.

They announced the six or eight people they hired to write the blogs, and of course I wasn't one of them. They weren't just going out and hiring rank amateurs—you know, actual bloggers. There was a couple of guys who were mixtape DJs; kris ex, who used to write for the dead tree version of XXL; XXL editor in chief Elliott Wilson; my go-to guy (for information on LCD rap) Noz; and a girl named Tara Henley.

And maybe a few other people. Who can remember, at this point. Literally a million people blogged for XXL at some point or another in the late '00s. Some they only kept around for a day or two.

Noz is an OG hip-hop blogger, but I think they only brought him on because he was trying to write for the dead tree version of XXL, and he just didn't have what it takes. One time they hired him to write an album review, and either they never ran it, or they ran it but then they never let him review anything else. It's not clear, and it would be impossible to say without finding where he wrote about it a long time ago. I think that's also how they found Tara Henley.

I never tried to pitch an album review or some shit to a magazine, because I never had any interest in writing for magazines. By the time I was in my mid 20s, I hadn't so much as picked up a rap magazine since I was a teenager. The first year or so I was in college, I would flip through The Source at a store called Hastings. I didn't have the $4 or whatever it cost. Eventually, I quit bothering. This was '99-2000. Rap music had seen better days.

Some of my Internets crew were upset that I hadn't been considered. My homeboy jimi izrael wrote a scathing post on his blog in which he charged Elliott Wilson with, and I quote, felonious cocksucking with attempt to swallow the evidence.

Damn.

jimi had already been involved in a back and forth with Elliott having to do with something he once wrote about Elliott's wife, Danyel Smith, former editor in chief of VIBE magazine.

It wasn't anything bad. He was actually very effusive in his praise for her writing—more than I personally felt was necessary. Elliott may have felt that jimi had some sort of interest in his wife. He may have been hoping, on a subconscious level, that jimi wanted to bang his wife, because she was getting on in years, and he wanted to think she was still desirable.

In a post about the time he was an intern at VIBE back in the mid '90s, jimi wrote about how Danyel Smith would purposely wear t-shirts a size too small, so as to accentuate her ginormous cans. I think she was in between men at the time. Which is not to say that a woman would only dress like that when she's trying to trap a man. Some women slut it up on a regular basis, for the ego boost.

Elliott must have Googled his wife's name and found jimi's post. He Googles himself a lot. He keeps an entire separate blog dedicated to cataloging mentions of himself in the press and elsewhere on the Internets. It's called Elliott Wilson: The Greatest Hip-Hop Journalist of All Time, or something along those lines.

The self-proclaimed greatest hip-hop journalist of all time responded to the fact that jimi izrael had the sheer balls to mention his wife's questionable mid '90s-era workplace attire by taking a few subliminal shots at him in his editorial in the next month's issue of XXL. You know that letter from the editor at the beginning of a magazine that no one ever reads, unless they're on an airplane and they've already everything else in the magazine twice?

That was Elliott's thing. If he had beef with you, he felt he was in competition with you, or you somehow upset him, he would insult you subliminally in his editorial in the next month's issue of XXL.

The way I became hip to this, and indeed the only reason I even bothered to check the editorial in that month's XXL in the first place, was because Elliott had beef with another guy I knew from the Internets, this guy Hashim. The two of them had been going back and forth for some time.

Hashim was another OG hip-hop blogger, who I guessed got tired of trying to make ends meet on the $1.70 per month you can make if you plaster your blog with Google Adsense and decided to go pro. He figured he would use his blogging expertise to land a quote-unquote real job. Who'd a thunkit. What Hashim lacked in technical expertise and ability to write he more than made up for in what Percy Miracles' date's father calls *chutzpah*.

He talked this site SOHH into starting a blog section. This was the original blog section of a hip-hop website, predating the late '00s-era XXL site by maybe a year. To his credit, I think they did have some success with it. Traffic to the blogs increased the number of pageviews, which increased the amount of income from banner ads. Cha-ching.

SOHH had been one of the original hip-hop websites, dating way TF back to the mid '90s. I think it started out as some sort of online hip-hop awards, for other rap sites of that era. It managed to withstand the late '90s-era bubble in hip-hop websites, when people like Russell Simmons and the guys from The Source decided to sink so much money in the Internets, because it never invested as much in original content. Its main feature was its popular message board, where the content was all user generated, as they say in the biz. Hiring a team of unknown kids to write blogs is the next level of profiting from user generated content.

Profiting primarily on content generated by any ol' d-bag with an email address and an Internets handle ended up being SOHH's downfall, as it turns out. As XXL was expanding its online operation, the SOHH boards were taking a turn for the worse. A group called the Pedo Army formed, for the purpose of trading pictures of underage girls. They would later claim that the name Pedo Army was a joke, but it looks like they really were trading pictures of underage girls. Albeit just barely underage. A more accurate name would have been Ephebo Army.

The term ephebophilia refers to a sexual preference for girls in their late teens—girls who are fully adult women for all intents and purposes ("intensive purposes"), except for the fact that they aren't necessarily legal to have sex with, depending on what state you're in. Most guys alleged to be pedophiles are really just ephebophiles, and I'm not sure if there's anything wrong with being an ephebophile per se. What normal, red-blooded American man isn't attracted to girls in their late teens? I'm not sure if I'd trust a guy who isn't.

But the Pedo Army thing just generated bad publicity. The thing that got SOHH driven from the Internets was when they picked a fight with the haX0r group Anonymous. I think this was the same group of kids who became famous for standing outside $cientology buildings with humorous protest signs, but who knows. They're anonymous by design. Hence the name. So it's not that I didn't research this thoroughly. (That's just a coincidence.)

Some young guy on the SOHH boards issued a challenge to the haX0r group to try to destroy SOHH. He wasn't anyone who owned or ran SOHH, it was just some random guy. In retrospect, it could have been someone from Anonymous pretending to be someone from SOHH. Like 9/11, this could have been an inside job. Allegedly.

At any rate, Anonymous responded by removing SOHH from the Internets. They did that thing they do where they overwhelm the server on which the site is located by bombarding it with too much traffic all at once. Which is really not that impressive to me, though of course I hope they never try anything like that with my site, or any of the other sites I check on the reg. The other thing they've had a lot of success with is guessing the answers to security questions for people's email accounts. That's how they hacked into both Sarah Palin and Mitt Romney's email. Does that even count as haX0ring?

Credit where credit is due: The haX0rs who took out SOHH somehow managed to hack into the site's back end and several people's email addresses, and I'm not sure how exactly they did it. I'm going to give them the benefit of the doubt and assume that they're that good. They hacked into one of the owners' email and supposedly found where he'd been stepping out on his wife. They scrawled racist graffiti and Nazi imagery on the site's front page. But probably just for the purposes of upsetting people. I doubt that they're really racist. The fact that they protest the Church of $cientology proves that they have an ultimately progressive agenda.

Hashim, who worked for SOHH as a sort of blogging coordinator, started plotting his next move. From what I understand, he approached XXL about doing for them what he'd done for SOHH, aside from the Pedo Army and the Nazi invasion. XXL was already considering revamping its online presence, since it was 2005, and its website still hardly consisted of anything other than an order form for the dead tree version of the magazine, and maybe that month's letter from the editor, if Elliott had something he was trying to promote that month. But why would anyone visit the site in the first place, if there wasn't anything there? They were doing it all wrong.

Talks between Hashim and the XXL brass eventually broke down. They must have realized that they could start a blog on their own just by going to any number of sites that hawk free blogging software and entering in a working email address. They decided to take his idea and run with it, saving themselves the 10s of thousands of dollars it would have cost to hire him. It's what the people who ran SOHH would have done if they had the sense God gave geese.

This of course didn't sit well with Hashim. He got back at XXL in a couple of ways. First of all, he had a shedload of pizzas delivered to the XXL offices. How he accomplished this, I'm not sure. Don't they have caller ID?

This was 2005. But credit where credit is due. I really do think Hashim is a smart guy, his technical expertise and his writing ability notwithstanding. Second of all, he started an entire separate media criticism blog at SOHH, seemingly for no other reason than to bait Elliott Wilson. That was what started the back and forth.

I went back and found some of those posts just now, as I'm writing this, to convince myself that it really did happen, and I see where Elliott may have taken a few subliminal shots at me in those '05-era editorials. I didn't realize this at the time, though it looks like Hashim did. (I told you the guy was smart.) This was a surprise to me, since I hardly knew who Elliott Wilson was at the time, and hence I didn't have any feelings towards him one way or the other. I had been under the impression that he didn't start to harbor any animosity towards me until much later, after I started working for him. Hmm...

I didn't pick up on it when I interviewed Elliott for my blog about this XXL Raps CD he was putting out, in the fall of '05, six months or so before I started working for XXL. If he had any problems with me, he didn't bother mentioning it. Later I was told that he was under the impression that I had a problem with *him*, because I never ran the interview. I never ran it because I lost the audio of it before I could transcribe it, because I'm madd lazy. I think he even once emailed me about it, and I told him as much. He must have thought I was lying, to protect my reputation as a guy who sits around in his underwear all day, developing tinnitus trying to hear those great mid '00s-era Hold Steady albums over a box fan I bought at my last day job, at K-Mart.

At any rate, our relationship at that point (pause) wasn't so strained that he didn't end up inviting me to blog for XXL, if only to stop the Internets from bitching. He had one of his young white boyservants contact me via instant messenger, to officially extend the invite. Of course I was interested, if only for the sheer thrill of being able to post something on the website of a major magazine. XXL back in those days sold more magazines from newsstands than Rolling Stone even (though only because the kind of people who copp XXL are too broke to spring for a subscription). It would be worth it just to see what I could get away with.

But I had to play it cool. I didn't want to seem too eager. I pretended to think it over. At that point, I learned more about XXL's plans to expand its online presence. In addition to the aforementioned Noz and Tara Henley, some of the other bloggers would include Elliott himself and longtime XXL scribe kris ex a/k/a Crispix a/k/a gunyogurt (nullus), a mixtape DJ named Sickamore, and DJ Drama. Sickamore I had been familiar with, because he has a somewhat unique name, but I had never heard of DJ Drama.

In fact, the name DJ Drama sounded ridiculous to me. It was too generic to be real, like if a rapper called himself MC Badass Black Guy. It's long been a theory of mine that you can tell when a rap group isn't trying hard anymore when they start giving their songs generic titles like "Keep It Moving." I think that was the name of a song from the fourth A Tribe Called Quest album. They were lauding themselves for their ability to keep it moving. They'd come a long way from "The Infamous Date Rape."

I copied the kid from XXL in an email to some other kids I knew from the Internets about how I'd been hired by XXL and what I'd learned about their for the site. I mentioned that some of the other bloggers would be some of the people who write for dead tree version of XXL, some people who tried to write for XXL but weren't quite good enough, Sickamore and some guy named DJ Drama. The kid from XXL replied that DJ Drama was a popular mixtape DJ in the South, as if there was something wrong with me for having never heard of him, and that he would appreciate it if I didn't disclose any more confidential information re: XXL. As if I'd sent out the security code to the XXL offices and the routing number for their bank account. Fine, I just wouldn't copy him on any more emails.

It was an awkward situation for me, because it's difficult enough for me to respond to that kind of reprimanding at places where I actually get paid. As long as my pay wasn't anything other than an ostensibly larger platform from which to mock failing rappers, I didn't need to hear that shit. And I worked for XXL for months and months before they paid me anything. Not even a box of cutout copies of XXL Raps CDs that I might have been able to sell back to record stores for pennies on the dollar, of which I'm sure there were plenty.

They only started paying me when they did because I arranged a sort of mini, low expectations bidding war for my services between XXL and SOHH. I saw it mentioned somewhere that SOHH had been paying their bloggers $500/month, and I thought to myself, shit, for $500/month it would be worth ditching XXL, a real music magazine, for SOHH, a sketchy website. That would damn near double my monthly income. To think of the things I could buy.

I hit up Hashim about ditching XXL for SOHH. He had the girl who ran SOHH email me. She offered me the standard $500. I was ready to take that shit, but I knew better than to bolt one job for another job without at least asking for a raise, from having a college degree in business. Never let it be said that my college education was a complete waste of my time. I forwarded the offer from SOHH to XXL, and they responded with twice as much. $1,000 a month. Can you believe it?

Instead of just taking that $1,000 straight to the bank, taking out a couple hundred in ones, and taking them over to the Eastside, I forwarded XXL's offer to SOHH. I was all ready to take that $1,000 (more money than I had at one time at any point in my life, up until that point), but I figured it couldn't possibly hurt to see if I could get even more than that. If I couldn't, I still had that $1,000.

SOHH responded with even more money than that, and a deal in which they would sell banner ads on my site and split the proceeds with me. I think the base pay, just to write a blog, was $1250/month. Who knows what I could have made altogether. I never have been able to make much money selling ads on my site. I would have taken it, and maybe I should have, but I just wasn't confident that SOHH would be around long term, despite the fact that it was already like 10 years old at that point. Turns out my decision was even more prescient than I realized at the time, if that's a correct use of the term prescient.

It's no wonder XXL didn't want me disclosing any of its confidential information. I might actually get paid for my work, as mandated by the UN's Universal Declaration of Human Rights, or whatever it's called, the same document people are referring to when they discuss the many, many times Israel has violated international law. It's not a law per se, but it should be.

Indeed, when XXL finally did start paying, I was told that I wasn't allowed to discuss my pay with any of the other bloggers—or anyone else, for that matter. I was told that this was because everyone else would be getting paid now, as well, but everyone wouldn't be getting paid the same thing, but to rest assured that I was getting paid more than everyone else, because I had a larger following. I believed that at the time, but now I suspect that the truth was the exact opposite. I was getting paid the same, if not less than everyone else, and they were playing on my outsize ego to keep me from asking questions.

Ultimately, as revealed in Howard Zinn's A People's History of the United States of America: 1492 to More or Less the Present, it's always the white man who's ripping you off (even if you're a white man yourself), but I'm man enough to admit that sometimes I should be credited with an assist.

# 10 PUPPET SHOW AND GHOSTFACE

As if the week I turned 25 couldn't get any better, I got a chance to go to a rap concert, the first rap concert I'd been to in years, maybe since I was in high school. I saw a few big rap concerts when I was in high school.

My old man used to have boxes at all of the big stadiums here in St. Louis and a row of seats behind home plate at Busch Stadium. Was it the worst childhood a guy could possibly have? No, it wasn't. But there comes a time when a man has to leave the nest, so to speak, and settle into an adulthood of poverty and failure. The sheer contrast between the two sets of circumstances made it that much more difficult. It's a wonder I survived.

Things would have been easier if I had been able to get into rap concerts for free, on the grounds that I'm an important hip-hop blogger. But, alas, that's just not how it works in rap music. In order to get into a concert for free, you have to work for a legit media outlet, like a newspaper.

Ben Westhoff, dog rape survivor, hit me up with the good news. Someone from Def Jam had offered him passes to a Ghostface Killah show over on the Eastside, in case he wanted to write something about it for the Riverfront Times. There was more than one pass, and I could have one if wanted to. Of course I did. The only place I wanted to go to more than a Ghostface Killah show in those days was a strip club, and we'd already been to a strip club.

Oddly enough, the venue for the Ghostface show was very close to one of the strip clubs we went to that night. It even shared the same parking lot. I think there was also a gas station in that parking lot. In fact, it could be the case that everything in Sauget, IL shares the same parking lot, like one big ne'er do well office park. The Monsanto plant and the minor league baseball stadium that serves the Luther Vandross sandwich, as seen on the Travel Channel's Man vs. Food, are within a stone's throw. No Madlib.

The gas station is located at the edge of the parking lot, near the highway. There's a cop who sits there in a parked car, but he's altogether unconcerned with catching drunk drivers. You can't get a DUI anywhere in St. Louis, except certain parts of the county on certain nights (like holidays), unless you're really driving crazy, and as previously discussed, Sauget has very few laws, and most of them have to do with what you're allowed to do with/to the strippers. One night, I almost got into a wreck pulling out of that parking lot. I was drunk as shit. The cop just waved me on my way. I guess no one had actually hit anything. He was just there making sure no one got carjacked.

Before the big show, we stopped at the gas station to grab a bite to eat. I wasn't hungry, he was. If I had been hungry, I would have stopped somewhere other than a gas station. Maybe he had counted on there being more dining options in Sauget. There was no minor league game that night, so the Luther Vandross sandwich was out of the question. In fact, I don't even think it was baseball season. Or do minor league teams play in March?

I of course suggested a Landshire sandwich. I don't know if they have them everywhere, but Landshire is a brand of sandwiches you can buy at a gas station here in the Midwest. They're coated with preservatives to the point where they can last for quite some time in one of those beer refrigerators. Your best bet is to heat it up in the microwave, but you won't die or anything from eating it cold. Even the hamburger. Or so I've been told.

They all have weird, silly, presumably tasting-sounding names. I used to know the entire line by heart, when I worked at K-Mart. Their top sandwich, their flagship, so to speak, was called the Nike, or the Super Nike. One time, when I was a kid, I asked my mom how there could be a sandwich called Nike when there was already a shoe called Nike. She said the sandwich probably predates the shoe. If that's the case, Landshire might want to have a talk with its lawyer.

I don't think Westhoff had ever had a Nike before. I handed one to him, and he turned it over and started looking at the nutrition facts. Bad move. Who looks at the nutrition facts of a sandwich from a gas station beer cooler? It might not even be food per se. I wouldn't trust those nutrition facts. Westhoff said he "couldn't eat just anything." He's one of the most judgmental people I ever met in my life. But that's alright. I'm accepting of other people's flaws. Sometimes it's important to be the bigger man, both literally and figuratively.

We had plenty of time to eat and probably do some of anything else, since of course a rap concert never starts on time. The Eastside never officially closes for business, so it's not so much a matter of if a rapper will show up as it is a matter of when. And some of these rappers make a little extra money charging local groups to pretend to be opening acts. The way it works is, you pay Ghostface or whomever $50, and you get the stage to yourself for like a half an hour at 5 PM, for a show that starts at like midnight.

In Sauget, this of course means a shedload of juggalo acts—young Insane Clown Posse fans from the suburbs, probably not far from where I grew up, who had to ask their parents for the $50. And maybe one or two black guys still holding out hope of being the next Nelly, 15 years after the fact. I don't want to say any names, in part because I don't know any of them well enough, and in part because I do believe it's important to support local artists. We all do our part. The RFT will sometimes report that a local rapper was "selected" as an opening act for a major label artist.

Or who knows, maybe it really is true that they won't just take anyone.

In between the juggalos and the car thieves there was a DJ, who I guess was an employee of the venue, so that things didn't get too quiet in between acts. Sometimes there's just the house music (not to be confused with the genre house music, whatever that is), and it's not at all appropriate. It's just whatever the guy who owns the place selects, and people who own concert venues never just happen to be fans of rap music. (What does that tell you about rap music?)

The DJ played several songs I enjoy, and no one seemed to give a shit. They weren't upset or anything, they were just kinda indifferent, too busy discussing pro wrestling, or whatever it is a juggalo enjoys other than ICP. Then the DJ threw on the song "What You Know," by T.I., and the crowd went wild, as if Holyfield had just won a fight. I didn't know what TF was going on. It couldn't have been the song, because the song's not that good.

But apparently it was. The DJ even did that thing where as soon as the song came to an end he played it again from the beginning. I know Funkmaster Flex has been known to do that with new songs by famous LCD rappers like Jay-Z. I used it do it with the Green Album by Weezer, even though it's not that good, just because it's so short and I didn't have any other plans. Sometimes I still do that with You Are Free by Cat Power, just because, if it's not already clear at this point from the text, I like to maintain a certain mood of sadness.

The last time I recall being at an event where the DJ did that was when "Gangster's Paradise" was at the height of its power, when I was in the ninth grade. Needless to say, that was the only dance I went to in high school, though I have since developed a certain appreciation for Coolio. Brittany Murphy in the movie Clueless was on to something, and not just drugs. "Fantastic Voyage" in particular. That's one thing the juggalos and I have in common. (I bet juggalos also enjoy pr0n.)

Eventually, several hours later, Ghostface Killah finally came out and destroyed. This was back when Ghost was at the height of his power. He was like "Gangster's Paradise" in 1995, except not nearly as popular. I was never as crazy about Fishscale as everyone else on the Internets, or anything he's done since, for that matter, but Fishscale I don't think had even been released. He was still doing a lot of shit from albums like Supreme Clientele and Pretty Toney, not to mention classic shit from the '90s. That was the time to see Ghostface live.

Cappadonna somehow managed to arrange plane fare to St. Louis. Or were they on a bus? Back in those days, he was notorious for showing up to concerts by other Wu artists to perform his verse from "Winter Warz," from Iron Man. He couldn't just do it at his own shows, because this wasn't 1998. LOL. Credit where credit is due: I saw a Cappadonna solo show once, and the shit was amazing. The man is a genius. Full stop.

## 11 I AM THE LEPRECHAUN

Some of the events of that night over on the Eastside became fodder for my first few posts as a professional hip-hop blogger. Alas, we never quite made it to the strip club that night. Those posts could have been even more interesting!

I wrote a post about how Ghostface's latter day major label rap career, with Def Jam, was destined to fail. Fishscale came out and sold like eight copies. It was more hyped on the Internets than Pretty Toney, which was a better album, the hype just didn't translate into sales. Rap album sales were starting to slide across the board, but his sales were down even if you adjust for music piracy, or whatever the problem seemed to be.

T.I.'s career was doing about as well as it ever has in the brief periods in between his many, many stints in prison. He had a movie coming out that week. His song "What You Know," which played over the end credits, was one of the top songs on the radio, and over on the Eastside, and it was also on his new album King, which, wouldn't you know, came out the same week. It was one of the last great fits of '90s-style corporate synergy.

Remember back when the movie studio, the record label, Entertainment Weekly, a late night TV talk show and probably a cereal company or some shit were all owned by the same corporation, and they would all get together to promote the same thing, like one of those shitty late '90s-era Joel Schumacher Batman movies? They made a lot of money promoting "urban" movies where they spent more money on the soundtrack than the movie itself. Some of the best rap music ever came from those soundtracks.

I wanted to find out for myself if any of the best rap music ever came from the new T.I. album, King. Or any good rap music, for that matter. I found a copy of the album for illegal downloading and illegally downloaded it. I joked at the time that I'd received a copy of the album from the label, to review, but of course Atlantic Records would never send me a T.I. album to review. But I'd like to state for the record that I've long since deleted that T.I. album, in case the RIAA is listening.

In fact, I haven't illegally downloaded an album in years. There's Spotify now, so why would I need to? But I hadn't illegally downloaded anything for a few years before there was a such thing as a Spotify. The albums I give a shit about these days are so few and far in between that I can buy like 10 albums a year, spend about $100, and not have to sweat breaking the law. Maybe a musician will even benefit lol jk. I stream anything I think I might like on NPR Music. There isn't anything I like that wouldn't be streamed on NPR Music. I have very good taste.

Good enough taste to know that King is a crap album. Even people who fuxwit T.I. don't really fuxwit King. It's not the T.I. album to get. I actually enjoy some T.I. myself. For my money, it's all about Paper Trail, which I believe was his most commercially successful album. Not to get all Patrick Bateman on you (yikes!), but I can see why it sold so well. It's goddamn enjoyable. It's the LCD rap album I recommend for people who don't usually fuxwit LCD rap. Like, if you've got a girl in the car or something.

I've only heard it like twice, four years ago, but I'm gonna go out on a limb and say that every song on Paper Trail is at least as good if not better than "What You Know." King has one or two songs that sound like limp "What You Know" knockoffs, and the rest is even worse. The absolute worst is a song called "Front Back," featuring UGK. It doesn't even sound like it belongs on the album. It sounds like a relic from the 1990s, before they had the technology to make songs that sound better than "Front Back."

Pimp C, who had recently been sprung from the pokey, spit a verse on "Front Back" that sounded eerily similar to every verse Mike Jones ever spit in his life, minus the part where he says his phone number. I'll admit that at that point in my life I was more familiar with Mike Jones than I was Pimp C. No Boutros. Probably still am. I missed the boat on UGK back in the '90s. I was too busy listening to great albums like Liquid Swords. I would see a UGK album given three mics in The Source, and I would just assume that was because it was mediocre.

The year or two leading up to Pimp C's release, Bun B spearheaded a campaign in which he went around wearing a Free Pimp C t-shirt, collecting any and every $200 fee someone was willing to pay him to appear on some no name brand mixtape. A new one would hit the Internets roughly every three days. He must have netted over $2,000 for fiscal year 2005. I can't say I wouldn't have done the same thing, if given the opportunity. I was in dire straits.

But it wasn't clear to me, listening to this T.I. album, why it was so urgent to get Pimp C out of jail, if that's all he had to offer. They could have just as easily left him in jail and it wouldn't have made me any difference. I said as much in my review, and I may have mentioned it in a post I wrote for XXL about the fact that I'd reviewed the new T.I. album. I used to like to kill two birds with one stone in that way. I'd review an album on my own blog, then I'd write about the fact that I reviewed an album on my own blog on my XXL blog. It was my own sort of low expectations corporate synergy.

Someone must have tipped Bun B off to the fact that I mentioned him in a post for XXL. I know he's on the Internets a lot, but I don't get the sense that he's much of a reader. He probably just likes to look at the titles of articles, any related pictures, audio and video. He's not unlike everyone else who ever visited the XXL website, in that sense. It's maddening, I tell you, writing for people who can't read. It's like trying to shout at the deaf girl from In the Company of Men. You can't just copy and paste gibberish, because the people who run the magazine *do* know how to read. Arggh!

Bun B was none too pleased. He took to the comments section and let loose with a diatribe in which he accused me of belonging to a country club and hiding behind bushes to throw rocks at people. He complained about people not wanting to support southern rap music, listed his real-hip-hop bona fides (pronounced bona feed-ace), including having met legit rappers like De La Soul and Kool Herc, and made thinly veiled threats to pop a cap in my ass. It was a thing to behold—like one of his retarded guest verses, but without the burden of having to rhyme the same three words over and over again. Someone should have given him $20 for it.

The Internets went nuts. Paul Wall never saw anything like this. Hundreds and hundreds of people left comments, as if anyone gave a shit. It was said that I had been "ethered." I was shocked. I hadn't expected anything like this. What did we ever do to these guys that made them so vio-lunt?

Bun B would later state that his concern was with Pimp C, who wasn't there to defend himself. I never got what he meant by that. I mean, I could see if Pimp C had still been in prison. But he had already been out for some time at that point. Hide your kids, hide your wife. How come he couldn't just log on to XXL and threaten to pop a cap in my ass himself?

From what I could gather, it had to be either one of two things. Either Pimp C had no idea when people were making fun of him via the Internets, because he didn't use them, because he didn't know how to read, or he *was* capable of using the Internets, and he did in fact know how to read, but he avoided using them, because he felt that just made it easier for the Illuminati to keep track of his whereabouts.

Pimp C has become a sort of patron saint of what's come to be known as Black People Twitter, with unemployed hoodrats at all hours of the night wondering whom he'd be accusing of being gay and/or a fake drug dealer, if only he hadn't overdone it with the sizzurp and being too fat to sleep properly. He used to write this column for Ozone magazine in which he'd lay into the likes of Ne-Yo, Russell Simmons and Young Jeezy. But he didn't really write it per se. He'd dictate it via cell phone to Ozone editor in chief Julia Beverly, my fantasy girlfriend.

It's also been suggested that the Illuminati had Pimp C rubbed out, perhaps for talking too much shit about Russell Simmons. They can't run the risk of Simmons' pre-paid debit card business being damaged. He must make a mint from that Rush Card. How else to explain the fact that he remains one of the wealthiest hip-hop moguls despite the fact that I haven't seen anyone in a Phat Farm t-shirt since I was in the sixth grade? Jay-Z, who's reported to be worth roughly the same amount, has a million different business ventures. Russell Simmons has relatively few.

If you check YouTube, you can find videos in which Pimp C's death is alleged to be the handiwork of the Illuminati. Pimp C was found dead in a hotel in LA, having succumbed to a combination of sizzurp and sleep apnea. He stopped breathing during his sleep, but he couldn't get up or change positions because of the sizzurp.

Herpes medicine was also found at the scene, according to Ben Westhoff, who must have read the police report in researching his book on southern rap, Dirty South, which apparently is thoroughly researched. Catching herpes must have made Pimp C paranoid about the prospect of dealing with suspect women. Part of his rants in Ozone had to do with so-called DL brothers, secret gay guys who occasionally sleep with women to keep up appearances, thus poisoning the pussy population, to use the parlance of the Pimp. (See what I did there?)

Years later, Bun B stopped by the XXL offices for some sort of online chat to be broadcast via Internets video. The first thing he did was inquire as to my whereabouts. Of course I didn't work out of the XXL offices. I never so much as visited the XXL offices the entire five years I worked there. In the chat, some young guy asked him to speak on the rumor that Pimp C had been taken out by the Illuminati, and Bun B went off on him. He thought the guy was trying to crack a joke, and this time Pimp C really couldn't defend himself if he wanted to, regardless of literacy.

I responded to Bun B's comment on my post with a subsequent post in which I thoroughly and systematically took apart Bun B's remarks and revealed them for the BS that they are. It would be one thing if all he did was call me names and threaten to kill me, be he also tried to make a point—and he failed.

Bun B had attempted to establish his hip-hop bona fides by naming several ostensibly credible members of the hip-hop community, including Kool Herc and De La Soul, that he's met in person, which, as I pointed out, is just silly. Any ol' dumbass could meet a famous rapper.

Having been in the game for something like 10 years now, I've met a few rappers myself. No one too famous, but how many rappers can claim to be genuinely famous these days? At the time, my celebrity encounters were relatively few and sometimes secondhand in nature. For example, I know a guy who once met Lisa Loeb. When I was in high school, I met one of the guys from the movie Hoop Dreams at the Missouri Black Expo. My little brother asked him if his father was still on crack. He said no, that was the other guy's father. After I graduated from college, I shared an apartment for a period of time with a guy who caddied for Bob Costas. I went to the same high school as at least one of the guys from the band Living Things (an obscure, early '00s-era major label White Stripes knockoff with supposed anarchist leanings, which is hilarious if you're familiar with the area), and the guy who wrote Hello, My Name Is Scott.

Bun argued that the South supported East Coast rappers for years, and now the East Coast didn't want to support southern rappers, because they were jealous, because the South was outselling the East Coast. The old Ricky Lake argument. "You just jealous!"

There is some truth to that. New York hasn't been right ever since West Coast rappers started outselling East Coast rappers, way the fuck back in the early '90s, let alone now that it's been surpassed by other parts of the country. New York's response has been, on the one hand, to bitch and moan about how whatever happens to be hot at any given moment isn't as good or as authentic as quote-unquote real hip-hop, which I of course tend to agree with, and on the other hand, to try to co-opt whatever happens to be hot at any given moment, which is ruining rap music. But it's neither here nor there to me personally, because I'm not from the East Coast.

Even if I had been, I don't believe in "supporting" artists by buying CDs. I always cringe when I see posts on blogs like Nah Right and the Smoking Section about how an artist has an album coming out in a few weeks, and we should all run out to Best Buy and cop it on CD (rather than just illegally download it) as a show of support. I do still buy music on occasion, but only to listen to, not to help fund the lifestyle of the people who created it. If the artist makes a few dollars from the deal, then so be it. If they don't, then maybe they need to find another way to make money. Guilt-tripping people into paying for a product that has no real intrinsic value is not an effective long term business strategy anyway. Take it from someone who went to business school.

Then there was the idea that I could somehow accidentally end up in the same situation Pimp C found himself in. Bun B didn't go so far as to say what that situation actually was, and it's never been clear to me how exactly Pimp C ended up in prison. When I was in college, I read on the message boards at okayplayer that he pulled out a gun on a woman in a mall. An AK-47 that he had tucked into a fur coat, in Texas in the middle of the summer.

This is at least partially untrue. I looked into it myself, because I believe in doing research, and I found that Pimp C was actually sent to prison for violating the terms of his probation stemming from the incident in the mall, not for the incident itself. You'd think that pulling out a machine gun in a mall alone would be enough to get you sent to prison, at least for a period of time, but I guess they don't see it that way in Texas.

And I'm assuming it was drugs that ultimately got him sent away. Those drug tests don't check for sizzurp, do they? That's more or less the same thing as cough syrup. You can't get fired from your job for taking cough syrup. What if you actually had a bad cough? I was once told by a guy who worked at the airport that they don't check for anything other than weed. You're actually encouraged to take coke, if you just have to get high. Unofficially, mind you. But they really do tell you that.

I guess it could have been a false positive due to the herpes medicine. Especially if he didn't bother to disclose the fact that he was on herpes medicine, out of embarrassment. How many people, when they're filling out their medical history at a doctor's office, include every single instance in which their dick itched for a few days after an encounter with a questionable woman? As long as it didn't fall off, that shouldn't count as part of your medical history.

At any rate, it seemed ridiculous to me that I could be at risk of accidentally pulling an AK-47 out of my fur coat and pointing it at a woman in a crowded shopping mall, traumatizing little kids on their way to Build a Bear. Because of course I would never go to the mall with an AK-47 tucked into my fur coat, because I own neither an AK-47 nor a fur coat. I rarely even go to the mall. Security at the mall near me has been extra suspicious of black people ever since that light rail train station was built across the street. If they tried to accuse me of stealing, I couldn't realistically claim to be there trying to buy something, because I don't have any money.

I rest on your face.

My Second Reply

My first response to Bun B went over so well that I issued a second response, in which I went further in depth re: how Pimp C ended up in prison. I didn't turn up any more information about what happened that day, but I figured I already had plenty to goof on, what with the AK-47 and the fur coat.

Someone in the comments section had responded that it wasn't just a woman Pimp C had pulled out a gun on, he'd pulled out a gun on an entire group of people, one of whom happened to be a woman. They wouldn't stop following him around. This seemed even more ridiculous to me than the idea of pulling out a gun on just the one woman. I think we can all relate to occasionally wanting to pull out a machine gun on a woman. The difference is, most of us don't happen to have a machine gun on us at the time. Most workplaces have rules against that.

Aside from just sizzurp and herpes medicine, Pimp C was known to rap about being on PCP. Back in the '60s, and as recently as when I was a kid in the late '80s/early '90s, PCP was famous for making people jump out of windows thinking they could fly. But I guess it manifests itself in different ways, depending on where you take it. There aren't as many tall buildings in Texas, because it's such a vast state. Real estate is plentiful. You don't have to build up, you can build out. I heard it's all strip malls as far as the eye can see. It sounds miserable. Hence the sense of ennui on the Arcade Fire's kinda great The Suburbs.

PCP has been known to make people see things. I joked that maybe Pimp C was under the impression that he was being chased through the mall by a group of leprechauns. At the time, there was a popular viral video of a crackhead somewhere down south, on the evening news, claiming to have seen a leprechaun in a tree.

After this second response, I received an email from one of Elliott's young white boyservants, ostensibly my boss (I was still working for free at that point), about how we had agreed that while my first response to Bun B was amusing, we should leave it at that. I was aware that he had emailed me after my first response to Bun B saying he thought it was amusing and that I should leave it at that, and that I had read it, but I didn't realize that that constituted an agreement on my part.

# 12 STANDING ON TOP OF HIP-HOP JOURNALISM

When I started blogging for XXL, I was told in no uncertain terms that I could write whatever I wanted to write and that no attempt would be made to tell me what to write or try to censor me. Maybe they felt they had to say that, because I was working for free, and so there was only so much BS I'd be willing to put up with.

Later, after they started cutting me a check, they sent me a letter to sign about how I wasn't allowed to issue any legal or medical advice. I'd been jokingly giving out legal and medical advice on the Internets for years, long before I was with XXL. I started calling myself Bol Guevara, MD, after an incident in which some kids found some sort of pro-life souvenir coin (no, really) near my desk at K-Mart, and I suggested they melt it down and use it as a scalpel to perform abortions. That didn't go over well. It wasn't the part of town for that kind of humor.

I think XXL just wanted to protect itself in the event of any potential lawsuits. If I told someone it was legal to kill a gay dog if it tried to rape your leg, and they did, XXL could always point to that document they had me sign. I went ahead and signed it, because I couldn't afford to run the risk of my check being delayed, but it didn't seem to make any difference. I continued to issue expert legal opinions, in part to see if anything would happen and in part "for my own personal amusement," and no one seemed to give a shit.

I would get censored every now and again, but only for the most random, arbitrary of reasons. Not because anything I said put XXL in a bad situation legally, but because it put someone in charge at XXL in a bad situation emotionally. I'd crack a joke someone didn't like, and they'd make me delete it, or they'd delete it themselves.

One time KRS-One and Marley Marl, who famously beefed with each other throughout the late '80s, put out a joint album. I joked that two old crackheads had gotten together to try to rescue hip-hop. Occasionally you do hear about crackheads rescuing people, I guess because crackheads are always out in the street and because crack gives you superhuman strength. Ol' Dirty Bastard once famously lifted a car off of a girl who had been run over. There was a sketch on Chappelle's Show about a crackhead who saved a baby who had been locked in a hot car by breaking the window in order to steal the radio.

Maybe a year before, after my beef with Kanye, I'd been contacted by a guy from Scratch magazine, XXL's one-time sister publication dedicated to DJing and rap music production. He was of course working on an article about rappers who don't write their own lyrics. I hadn't been familiar with Scratch. He said I should check it out; it was a better magazine than XXL, which was known at the time for its constant coverage of Interscope artists like Eminem and 50 Cent.

I picked up the then-current issue of Scratch, with Nas and DJ Premier on the cover. I'm not sure how great of a magazine it was, but at least there weren't any articles about 50 Cent. In fact, I think that was the idea behind Scratch: to placate people who know from good rap music, once they started making so much money putting 50 Cent on the cover of XXL every other month.

I was bored as shit at the time, so I ended up reading that issue of Scratch cover to cover. There was an interview towards the end with Marley Marl, who I guess was trying to get his career back in order. They asked him where he had been since his career started to cool off, back in the early '90s, and he admitted to having been on crack.

He had been rumored to be on crack as far back as the mid '80s. KRS-One had alluded to it on the legendary Juice Crew dis "The Bridge Is Over." Come to find out, that was the most accurate dis song of all time. The part about Roxanne Shante also turned out to be true. She got caught in a lie claiming she forced Warner Bros., via a clause in her contract, to put her through medical school, where she became a shrink. I think she was going around delivering motivational speeches. Never believe anything that's said in a motivational speech.

KRS-One himself has never been on crack, as far as I know. He's just crack-ish. He used to be homeless. He's known for making off the wall statements.

XXL editor in chief Elliott Wilson is a big fan of KRS-One. He used to think KRS-One was the greatest rapper of all time. In fact, KRS-One is number one on a list of the greatest rappers of all time in Ego Trip's Book of Rap Lists, to which Elliott Wilson contributed. Now Elliott considers Jay-Z the greatest rapper of all time. Jay-Z was somewhere in the lower reaches of the top 10 of the Ego Trip list, from the late '90s, as I recall. KRS-One's creative output hasn't gotten significantly worse since the late '90s, and Jay-Z's creative output hasn't gotten significantly better, but Jay-Z has made a lot of money, and Elliott Wilson considers that an important factor in determining who's the greatest rapper of all time.

A few hours after I clicked publish on my post, someone emailed me and told me that it needed it to be censored. While the use of the term crackhead to refer to KRS-One and Marley Marl was arguably accurate, Elliott Wilson considered it disrespectful, and so I needed to either come up with another title or get rid of the post altogether. After consulting with a member of my Internets crew, Straight Bangin', I decided that the best course of action would be to change the term crackhead to leprechaun, in tribute to the crackhead who claimed to see the leprechaun in the tree, in that YouTube video.

A mere matter of days later, Marley Marl had a heart attack. People in the comments section wondered how someone in his mid 40s could just randomly have a heart attack like that. It just goes to show how BS censorship leads to rampant ignorance.

There were few posts like that, in the beginning of my career with XXL, so to speak, where I was forced to change a word or get rid of a passage, or else delete the entire post, lest someone with a crack problem be called a crackhead. Later I would be known for having a number of posts mysteriously disappear from the Internets shortly after they were published.

My first post flushed down the memory hole had to do with a guy named Chaz "Slim" Williams. This guy was a legendary career criminal who of course found a place for himself in the business side of rap music. One day I was checking Radar, a site that hardly had anything to do with rap music, and I found an article about how 50 Cent had threatened to no longer pose for the cover of XXL, because he was pissed that they had run an article on Chaz "Slim" Williams, who may or may not have had something to do with that time 50 Cent was supposedly shot nine times.

Radar, at the time, was an actual magazine that trafficked in media gossip, a sort of dead tree version of Gawker. Obviously it wasn't a very good business idea. I heard it was somehow owned by Jesse Jackson, who must be in the Illuminati. (Or maybe he caught them discriminating against black people and guilt-tripped them into giving him equity—I don't want to speculate.) It's since been sold to a tabloid newspaper, which uses the website to run a lot of stories on the Octomom.

Word on the street was that 50 Cent told XXL that they weren't allowed to run a story on Chaz "Slim" Williams, before it went to print, and they did anyway, so now he was threatening to never again appear on the cover of XXL. Which was of course bad news for XXL, since 50 Cent was turning up on the cover seemingly every few months back in those days. He had been instrumental in XXL's success and ultimate triumph over its chief competitor, The Source.

XXL famously overtook The Source once and for all the month 50 Cent, Dr. Dre and Eminem, all Interscope artists, appeared on the cover of XXL along with the headline "The Real Hip-Hop Is Over Here" (a reference to a song by KRS-One, from his beef with St. Louis' own Nelly), thus signaling the fact that Interscope had pulled all of its ads from The Source and prohibited its artists from appearing on the magazine's cover.

The Source was as good as done. Eminem and 50 Cent probably sold as many albums back in those days as the rest of the rappers combined. Eminem alone sold more albums in the 2000s than any other artist.

Eminem's manager Paul Rosenberg, who holds a lot of sway with both Interscope Records and SiriusXM, ordered Interscope to stop running ads in The Source, after The Source had turned up audio of Eminem calling a black girl he went to high school with the dreaded n-word. Eminem had a crush on this black girl, and he must have gotten upset with her when she went and got it on with a black guy, someone who had what it takes to really satisfy her, if you catch my drift. And so Eminem made a recording of himself calling her the dreaded n-word.

Well, that's mostly speculation on my part (you can tell I spend a lot of time on the Internets), but the part about the tape of Eminem calling a black girl the dreaded n-word definitely is true. The Source printed up copies of it and distributed them along with an issue of the magazine filled with attacks on Eminem. The cover featured an image of Source co-owner and marketing executive Benzino clutching Eminem's decapitated head. There was an article about how white people were trying to take over rap music the same way Elvis stole rock and roll from black people.

Benzino is at least half-white. His father, who appeared in one of his videos, is melanoma white a/k/a Sophie Dee white. Most white people in Boston are. They must not get a lot of sun in that part of the country. I can't claim to be familiar with his mother, but I think he does consider himself part-black, and I'm willing to give him the benefit of the doubt. I'm magnanimous like that.

At any rate, he's white enough that he set off Eminem's radar. Eminem's YT sense started to tingle, if you will. Eminem has had beef with most white rappers at some point in time or another. But it's not just an Eminem thing. White rappers can't stand other white rappers. Name me a white rapper, and I'll name you another white rapper he's had beef with. I think it's because when a white rapper sees another white rapper who looks corny, which is of course often, it makes him feel self-conscious. It's like when black people see other black people acting a damn fool in public.

Then there's the fact that beefing with other white rappers doesn't carry with it the same risk as beefing with a black rapper. If you beef with a black rapper and you win, and his career is destroyed, people might get upset with you for putting yet another black man out of work. Rap music fans are a lot more concerned with how much money a rapper makes than whether or not his music is any good. As Curtis "Booger" Armstrong once explained, in a sluggish economy, you don't fuck with another man's livelihood. And it's always a sluggish economy for black people. Whereas, if you destroy a white rapper's career, you probably just did the world a favor anyway. LOL

Elliott Wilson had been an editor with The Source back in the late '90s. This was after it lost its credibility, by letting Benzino strongarm his way into co-ownership but before it completely went off the rails, with the failed online venture, the beef with Interscope, the sexual harassment lawsuits, so on and so forth. Elliott was the music editor. The music editor is the guy who assigns the actual mic ratings for albums. If you saw a review in The Source in the late '90s and you thought it was some ol' bullshit, it's his fault.

He claims to have left The Source because a mic rating was changed on an album by Kurupt. This seems ridiculous to me. I used to read The Source back then, and I can't recall any albums by Kurupt receiving an especially high rating. And I can't imagine Elliott Wilson having wanted to give an album by Kurupt an especially high rating. Kurupt himself wouldn't give an album by Kurupt an especially high rating. It wouldn't be worth it. No one would believe it anyway. You don't just throw away a job like that over an album the artist's own mom probably didn't buy.

Similarly, much of the original staff of The Source, from back when it had credibility, left all of a sudden back in the mid '90s, supposedly because co-owner Dave Mays went behind their backs and inserted an article about Benzino's group back then, The Almighty RSO, right before it went to print. The Almighty RSO wasn't relevant enough for their usual high standards. A few of those people went on to found XXL.

Up until that point, Harris Publications, the company that owns XXL, had primarily been in the business of publishing gun magazines. They somehow managed to find a way to publish something ridiculous like 15 different magazines all having to do with guns. I guess different people use guns for different purposes. Criminals use guns to commit crime. The police use guns to enforce the law, i.e in case any criminals are still around when they show up half an hour after a crime took place, at the same place where a crime always takes place. Hmm...

Harris Publications must have sensed a unique marketing opportunity in publishing both XXL and Guns and Ammo for Law Enforcement.

The people who left The Source to found XXL ended up leaving XXL after a year or two, crying racism, if you can imagine. But not because Harris Publications was running, on the one hand, a magazine teaching black kids to be criminals, and on the one hand, a magazine showing law enforcement which guns to shoot them with. Because supposedly Harris Publications had offered them equity and then reneged.

As is the case with the exodus from The Source, I'm not sure if I buy the official story. I mean, I'm sure they would have *liked* a stake in the company, and I'm sure the old CACs who owned XXL were not at all interested in signing over part of the company to some people from a rap magazine, but who ever heard of a company randomly promising to give its employees equity? K-Mart doesn't even let you own that red vest they make you wear. You have to give that back when you leave.

If they had been promised equity, it would have been mentioned in some sort of contract, and Harris wouldn't have had any choice but to follow through with it. (I'm allowed to issue expert legal opinions in my own book, right?)

The word went out in hip-hop journalism circles. Harris Publications is a racist company, and any black writer who took a job with XXL would be viewed as a sellout.

Enter Elliott Wilson. It had been a while since he had been with The Source, as music editor. Ego Trip, the hip-hop journalism collective of which he was once a member, got a deal to write that Book of Rap Lists. He poured himself into working on it, for a period of time, while the rest of the Ego Trip crew worked for other rap magazines, but now it was completed. He had run up a lot of credit card debt on '90s-style hip-hop clothes and visits to a strip club, where he was a regular.

He was at a low point in his life. He had somehow managed to be diagnosed with high blood pressure, despite the fact that he was neither very black nor particularly old. He must have been eating off of that buffet in the strip club. They put a lot of salt in the food so that they don't have to change the pans over as often. He tried playing basketball, for exercise, but he was too slow to play with guys his own age, so he had to join a senior citizen league. He also went on prescription meds that made him pee frequently. He could have taken another pill, to make him pee less often, but that probably would have just led to some other side effect. It's a vicious cycle. He was at risk of becoming the hip-hop journalism equivalent of Fat Elvis. He even kinda looked like Fat Elvis.

A meeting was held in which Elliott consulted with some of the other guys from Ego Trip (which was secretly owned by a white guy). Elliott cried, there was a group hug, and it was decided. Elliott would take the job with XXL, sellout accusations be damned. Those credit card bills weren't going to pay for themselves.

At XXL, Elliott set about seeking revenge for the great injustice that was being forced to give a Kurupt album three and a half mics when he felt it only deserved an even three. I don't think I need to tell you where this is headed. Elliott started taking shots at Ray Benzino and The Source in his monthly letter from the editor. Benzino of course didn't take very kindly to this, and from what I understand, at a certain point, he sent some people to the XXL offices looking for Elliott. Fortunately, Elliott didn't get dropped from the roof of the building or anything. I mean that sincerely.

In an issue of The Source, maybe the same issue with the headless Eminem on the cover (I was in college when this was going on, in the middle of nowhere), there was a Playboy-style centerfold with a big picture of Elliott or someone from XXL—a dorky, pasty CAC—being snapped in two by the kind of huge black guy who looks like he has sex with a lot of guys in prison.

Was the black guy meant to represent Benzino? Then why wasn't he light skinted? White rappers may suffer from a disorder along the lines of the one where perfectly fapworthy women see themselves as being fat when they look at themselves in the mirror. A woman's body can always be a little bit better than it is, but women who suffer from body dysmorphia, or whatever it's called, are rarely the ones who really need to be concerned. The fact that they see themselves as being fat shows that they still give a shit about their looks.

The more you suffer, the more it shows you really care. Right?

Clearly, The Source was spinning out of control. Benzino was being allowed to run amok. They famously borrowed $30 million to build a website. Which is ridiculous, because why would you spend money to build a website? The editor in chief at the time, Kim Osorio, was rumored to have become something of a community bicycle for rappers.

By the time I was with XXL, I don't think there was any real risk of any rappers threatening not to pose for the cover. XXL was the only game in time. I'm not even sure if The Source was still in business at that point. It went away for a period of time. 50 Cent could have taken his proverbial marbles and went home to Mike Tyson's old house in Connecticut, but it wouldn't have done him any good. He needed as much free publicity as he could get. Hence the fake beef with Kanye. Curtis came out later that year and never did quite go platinum, as far as I know. I remember checking week after week, to see how long it would take. Finally, I just gave up. Kanye's Graduation, released the same day, sold a million copies out the gate.

I think Elliott just didn't want people finding out about the ridonkulous level of shenanigans that take place behind the scenes in hip-hop journalism. He knew that if he pulled the plug on my post, none of those kids would ever find out any of that information, even though it was freely available elsewhere on the Internets, which is where I found it. A lot of this shit I didn't even find out until years later, when Elliott was let go from XXL and he got pissed at me for uncovering some of the secrets behind the amazingly corrupt RapRadar a/k/a RapPravda (but let's not get ahead of ourselves). It's not enough for information to just exist somewhere on the Internets. It takes someone with vision to compile it into a damning narrative.

# 13 ANOTHER MAN'S FREEDOM FIGHTER

I once at a Cheesecake Factory and a Chinese buffet on the same day. It may have been the single greatest day of my life, just in terms of restaurant food consumption.

Once I started getting paid to blog for XXL, I'd hit up a local Chinese buffet for lunch every now and again. It was in a strip mall between a pet store and one of those party supply stores. I always felt kinda weird eating at a Chinese restaurant next door to a pet store, but what are you gonna do? The price was very reasonable.

Do the pets for sale at a pet store ever die before some poor kid can come and buy them, and if so what do they do with them? Just toss them in a dumpster out back? I know PETA kills thousands upon thousands of pets per year, for humanitarian reasons, and keeps them locked in a freezer, in case they can figure out how to reanimate them, like baseball great Ted Williams.

It's a moot ("mute") point now, since the pet store has gone out of business. The Chinese place has since come up in the world, no longer situated next door to the last business it could possibly want to be next door to. Maybe the price of meat has gone up slightly (lol jk), but I'm sure a lot more people feel safe eating there.

But I can't say for certain, because I haven't been there in a while. I've been out of a job for some time now, so I'm not eating in restaurants nearly as often, let alone somewhere as fancy as a Chinese buffet, but I'd already stopped hitting this Chinese buffet before I was out of a job, because I didn't like the way I was being treated.

I wasn't even sweating the passive aggressive signs all over the place, or that thing they do where they set your check on the table after you've had three full plates, or the way they seem to withhold fresh crab rangoon until it looks like you're ready to leave. That kind of BS I can deal with. I'm a veteran of dealing with contentious situations in Chinese buffets from having braved crab leg night, on Sundays, at the Chinese buffet in Chicken Switch. That shit was like my own personal 'Nam.

The thing that did it for me was when they started hiring Mexicans. Not that I'm against Mexicans sneaking into our country and stealing our jobs. I'm not a racist or anything. Open the border up, as far as I'm concerned. But someone needs to explain to them that there's a certain way that you treat people.

One of the Mexicans working at this Chinese buffet somehow managed to get promoted from occasionally bringing out a new tray of cream of sum yung gai and setting it in the steam table to walking around the dining room with a pitcher of ice water, filling people's glasses. I was happy to see that, because I love nothing more than to see a minority get ahead in life. Apparently, there was no concern that people would see him and start to question the authenticity of the food on the buffet.

One day I was hitting the buffet especially hard. I was something like five full plates deep, going for a sixth. And can you believe this Mexican guy gave me a weird look, like there was something wrong with me for trying to get my full $8 worth? I was actually less concerned with the blatant disrespect than I was with the fact that he seemed to give a shit about how much I was costing the restaurant, as if it mattered to him personally. As if he owned the place. I'm sure he got paid the same either way. As long as the place didn't go out of business. And it's not like I ate *that* much. I'm not even sure if I ate $8 worth of food, what with the quality of food they serve in those places.

Is there a Mexican equivalent for what Malcolm X termed the house negro (as opposed to the field negro), the slave who was allowed to live in the house with his master, who eventually came to identify with his master rather than his own people? There must be some sort of equivalent phenomenon going on with Mexicans in the restaurant business. You let one of them walk the dining room floor with a pitcher of water and the next thing you know he hates black people more than the white guy who owns the place.

Fortunately, only but so many of them will ever be allowed out of the kitchen. The trend these days is towards hiring women with gigantic cans and tiny shirts to fill up your water. So-called breastaurants are one of the only growing segments of the restaurant industry. There was an article about it in the Wall Street Journal. It has to do with the state of the economy. People can't afford to go to restaurants nearly as often. If I'm gonna spend upwards of $12, I can't have just any ol' woman bringing me my lunch. I'll go somewhere else.

It's only a matter of time before someone creates a website or an app ranking restaurants and waitresses by cup size, firmness and jiggle. We'll know exactly where to go, and when, to get our full $12 worth, so to speak. I can't build it myself, because I don't have the tools or the talent, but if someone else builds it I think it's only right that I'm at least named as the guy who came up with the idea. Really, I should receive some sort of financial compensation.

If a Chinese buffet doesn't serve anything for dinner that they don't serve for lunch, there's no point in paying the two dollar surcharge to eat there during the evening. I think they count on people not being able to stuff themselves with salt, sugar and fat-laden Chinese food to the point of debilitating themselves in the middle of the day, because they have to work for a living. This of course was of no concern to me personally.

I think the lunch and dinner buffet, with minimal tip (just rounding up to the nearest one, since it's a buffet), will run you $8 and $10 respectively. That extra $2 doesn't buy you shit other than being able to eat during the evening. This place doesn't do much, if any seafood. Unless you count crab rangoon, which I believe is just cream cheese. Shrimp flavored ramen noodles probably has more seafood in it.

What I would do is plan an entire 24 hour period around having lunch at a Chinese buffet. Maybe spending $8 for lunch is kinda expensive, for a professional "content provider," but I knew that if I ate enough at lunch, I wouldn't have to eat again until noon the next day. So it was really only like spending $4 for lunch. Or maybe even less than that. I may have been saving money by having lunch at a Chinese buffet.

It was the fifth anniversary of 9/11. What better day to gorge yourself on shitty Chinese food? But I didn't plan it that way. It just kinda worked out that way. I rolled off of the couch and wrote whatever I needed to write that day, so I could be at the buffet when it opened at 11, when the chicken was still kinda crisp, or as crisp as it was ever gonna be anyway.

On my way there I get a call from Brendan, my would-be boss at XXL. He says that Lupe Fiasco has been allowed to write a guest post for the XXL blog, and I'm gonna want to read it. I might need to craft some sort of response. And that was all that he told me. Hmm... I was intrigued, but obviously I wasn't about to turn the car around to read something written by Lupe Fiasco. I'm not sure what it would take to get me to turn around on the way to a Chinese buffet.

So I get back from the Chinese buffet, stuffed to the gills, covered in flop sweat, smelling of broccoli and MSG. I log on to the XXL website, and wouldn't you know Lupe has written a post calling me the dreaded n-word and threatening to "jump off in my ass." It's a good thing he wasn't there at that very moment. My stomach could have exploded, like the guy in that movie Se7en.

Apparently, he was upset about something I had written earlier that summer, about how Lupe had threatened to retire from rap music before his first album had even been released as a publicity stunt, upset that songs from the album had been leaked to the Internets.

I think what happened was, someone from the label had informed him that there wasn't much of a business case for releasing Food and Liquor, because not enough people liked that song "Kick, Push," and so he decided to pretend as if the reason the album wasn't being released was because a few songs from the album had trickled onto the Internets. Meanwhile, every rap album there ever was has been leaked to the Internets ahead of its release date, going back to the days of I Am... by Nas and Murda Muzik by Mobb Deep, way TF back in the '90s. Jay-Z famously stabbed Lance "Un" Rivera for bootlegging copies of Vol. 3. Gravy poured from the wound. The only rap album that made it anywhere near its release date without being leaked to the Internets was Watch the Throne, and it was protected by the Illuminati. Whoever finally did upload it to the Internets was probably the victim of a vicious anal rape (is there any other kind?) by a shapeshifting lizard and/or Satan incarnate.

I saw Lupe perform that summer at one of those outdoor music festivals in Chicago. The response was tepid at best. He only had one song anyone had ever heard of, and he could only perform it for so long. The album was probably supposed to be out at that point, but it had been pushed back until the label could figure out a way to generate interest. Lupe announced that he was working on songs with Three 6 Mafia and Jill Scott, and I thought to myself, tha fuck? No one who wants to buy an album with a song by Three 6 Mafia on it also wants to buy an album with a song by Jill Scott on it, and vice versa. Why would Lupe want to record with either of them?

Three 6 Mafia were hot off of their Oscar win for the song "It's Hard out Here for a Pimp," or whatever it was called, from the truly excellent Hustle and Flow. They weren't turning down offers for anything. Jill Scott is a chick R&B singer, and you know how people love rap songs with chick R&B singers on them. Jill Scott wrote that song "You Got Me," which was the closest thing The Roots ever had to a hit, but they didn't want her to sing it in the video, because she's a disgusting tub of lard, so they got the lovely Erykah Badu instead. Something similar happened in the mid '90s with the song "Doin' It" by LL Cool J.

I set about crafting my response, highlighting the fact that Lupe, like Will Smith, had been known for not having to curse in his raps to sell records, and now here he was calling me a bitch-ass dreaded n-word and threatening to put a shoe on me, and also the fact that obviously he didn't have anything else to write about, and he was using my popularity at XXL to try to generate interest in his shitty album. The latter would become increasingly clear as his week-long guest blogging stint continued.

The phone rang. It was rare that I received two phone calls in the same week, let alone the same afternoon. Unfortunately, I wasn't getting a lot of phone calls from lovely young ladies asking me to come over and put my finger on them. It was my mom. She said it was my cousin's birthday, they were having dinner at the Cheesecake Factory, and I could go if I wanted to. Can you believe it? The one day that week I was planning to have lunch at a Chinese buffet. It was the fifth anniversary of 9/11 and a Monday. This was no time to celebrate your birthday at the Cheesecake Factory.

But of course I wasn't about to turn down free Cheesecake Factory. There was maybe a six hour span between when I got back from the Chinese buffet and dinner at the Cheesecake Factory. I wasn't planning on eating anything at all for dinner, but I figured I could probably still eat a decent-sized meal, if I had to. I'm an extremely large brother, and I'm not one of these poor bastards who somehow got to be ginormous without eating. If anything, I probably eat more than the average guy my size. I don't have the worst metabolism in the world, thank God.

How else could I have finished off an entire meatloaf entree that night at the Cheesecake Factory? The meatloaf might be the most ridonkulous thing you can possibly order at the Cheesecake Factory, just in terms of the amount of food you get. The sesame chicken is worse *for* you, and probably worse than anything else you could possibly eat in a restaurant, but that's because Chinese food will kill you. It doesn't have nearly the intimidating presence of the meatloaf entree. The amount of mashed potatoes they give you alone is probably more than the single largest container of mashed potatoes you can buy at a Costco. I don't think they expect anyone to actually finish it. It's part of their shtick.

Fast forward a few weeks. Food and Liquor was sliding down the charts like buttery mashed potatoes down a fat man's throat. I'd gotten into an argument with a guy who tried to claim that the US wasn't at war with Islamic fascism, because I think technically our goal was to look for the terrorists, or make sure Saddam didn't have any nuclear weapons. Technically, we weren't even at war. We were just over there looking for shit. The poor bastards who died in Iraq and Afghanistan didn't die in a war per se. The US hasn't been in an official, according to Hoyle war since maybe World War II. My argument was that we were in fact at war with with Islamic fascism, because the president went on TV and said we were at war with Islamic fascism. Duh.

The thing is, some people object to the use of the term Islamic fascism because they find it to be racist against people from the Middle East, similar to how the term illegal immigrant has now come to be viewed as racist against Hispanic people. What they did may have been against the law, but is it necessary to say that something is against the law, just because it is in fact against the law, especially when some people think it shouldn't be against the law? I kid the Hispanic people, but I can kinda see where they're coming from. An illegal immigrant already had to sneak into this country illegally, just to stand outside in the hot sun all day picking fruit. As long as it doesn't have any bearing on the actual policy, which I'm sure it won't, why not allow him to call himself whatever he'd like to be called? Same difference. Similarly, I can't imagine that the terrorist wing of Islam takes any solace in knowing that PC types on the Internets don't think the US is at war with them.

I got to thinking about these issues, I stumbled upon the artwork for Lupe Fiasco's Food and Liquor, and it got me to thinking. What exactly does Lupe mean to suggest here? There was Lupe, suspended in space with a blank expression on his face like someone had erased the contents of his brain and trained him to kill, like Matt Damon in the Bourne Identity, surrounded by technology, which I know the terrorists don't like (which, ironically enough, I'm sure has hampered their efforts in obtaining a nuke), and then there was title of the album, in some sort of Islamic font. I was already suspicious of Lupe, because one of the girls I worked with at XXL had praised him for being against scantily clad women dancing in rap videos, and I figured it probably wasn't because he's a particularly progressive person, especially after he threatened to jump off in my ass. Is Lupe against women shaking their asses in rap videos because he thinks the idea is played out, or because he thinks women should have at least 3/4ths of their bodies covered at all times?

I raised these and other issues in a post for XXL called "Lupe Fiasco, jihadist." I'll admit, it wasn't my best work, which I regret in retrospect because it became so widely read. Like a lot of the crap I was churning out back in those days, it was filled with more conjecture than actual research or storytelling. It started out with the idea that Lupe Fiasco could be a pro-terrorist rapper, but nobody realized it, because no one really listens to his music, and it used that as a jumping point to discuss whether or not he is in fact with the terrorists. One of the main things I questioned, and one of the things people really seemed to object to, was what group of Islam Lupe belongs to, the actual religion as it's practiced in the Middle East, or what I termed prison Islam. Apparently, members of the latter don't like to think that there's much of a difference between the two. But if that's the case, then why did Malcolm X have to switch from the one to the other? #logic

It could be that people just objected to the term prison Islam. Again, nomenclature issues. But trust that by "prison Islam" I didn't mean anything other than the fact that it's often picked up in prison. Christianity is often picked up in prison as well, but the Christianity you pick up in prison doesn't differ much if at all from the BS you can pick up on the outside. It wasn't just randomly invented in the 1930s. I didn't mean to suggest anything negative about its members by pointing out the fact that many of them have been to prison. I understand the fact that the prison-industrial complex is a scam to keep black men out of the work force. So many black people are supposedly in prison for drugs, meanwhile the only people on drugs are white people. The black man couldn't afford to do drugs if he wanted to. Don't hate the player, hate the game.

But try talking any sense into crazed Muslim Internets PC activists. It's no use. The comments section went nuts with people calling for my head. Probably literally! A Muslim guy who had been in cahoots with Clyde Smith, both of whom had been jealous of my career so to speak as a professional blogger, suggested a boycott of XXL. A Muslims in hip-hop group based on MySpace took them up on their offer. They started circulating a memo all about how I'm racist against Muslims, how I had unfairly attacked Lupe, how XXL should be driven out of business by a boycott, so on and so forth. It had the names, addresses and phone numbers of some of the white people who owned and ran XXL. There was no way this could end well.

I figured out the address of their little group on MySpace, where they were plotting on me, but I couldn't access it, because it was set to private. This was back when people were still using MySpace. It seemed ridiculous to me that a group that may or may not have been with the terrorists could have a space online where they could plot against people and we wouldn't even know what they were saying—though I guess Homeland Security, if necessary, could figure out a way to hack into MySpace, or just get MySpace to hand over people's private information.

And that's when some young guy hit me up on MySpace. He said he was a Muslim, and a fan of the blog, and he just so happened to be a member of this group that was plotting on me. He said he could probably get me a login for this group, so I could make sure they weren't trying to blow up my car, like in the movie Casino (a popular tactic in the Middle East). He also said a lot of weird, unnecessary homoerotic things and more or less admitted to being on the DL. It was the weirdest thing. It was almost like he wanted me to somehow come save him from Islam, like Katie Holmes trying to escape from Tom Cruise and the Church of $cientology.

I sat and eagerly awaited any further information from this Muslims in hip-hop group, or anything else this crazy guy might send me (nhjic). Instead, I received a message from the guy's wife, sent via his MySpace account. I guess she was monitoring his MySpace account and saw where he had offered to undermine the terrorists' cause for me and also admitted to being secretly gay. She apologized, said that there wouldn't be any further information forthcoming, and that the guy was "confused" and "going through some issues."

As if things couldn't have gotten any weirder.

And that was the last I heard from either of them. I checked a couple of times, and I don't think the guy so much as logged into his MySpace account again. Hopefully nothing bad happened to him. I know it's not considered PC to suggest that some Muslims are intolerant people, but let's keep it real. Some Muslims don't play that shit. I shudder to think what the punishment is for being on the DL. In retrospect, maybe I should have forwarded that conversation to the authorities, just in case. If that guy wants to play with another guy's balls, he should be free to play with another guy's balls. This is America. No homo.

# 14 DAMN, GINA!

I once wrote a post about Ray J that resulted in my own blog being completely removed from the Internets. The whole entire thing. Even the parts that didn't have anything to do with Ray J. Then I mentioned it in a post for XXL, and that post had to be removed for a period of time, but for an entirely different reason. I swear, that Ray J is nothing but bad luck. Whitney Houston had to find out the hard way.

When I was in college, I read a rumor on a message board that Ray J was getting it on with a lot of women. This was long before the fake sex tape with Kim Kardashian or the proposed book about how he had made sweet, passionate love to literally thousands of women by the ripe old age of like 26. It must have been true, if it had spread to the parts of the Internets where I could be found back in those days without Ray J himself trying to propagate it. He must have banged some guy's sister, and that guy told another guy about it, and the other guy was like, "Damn, he banged my sister, too!"

This was difficult for me to accept for a couple of reasons. First of all, of course, this was at a time when I wasn't having as much success with women as I would have liked. Well, I'm not sure if it's ever possible to have the amount of success with women that I'd like, but suffice it to say that I wasn't having an amount of success with women that would seem fair. If Ray J gets to bang thousands of women, I should be guaranteed at least some tiny percentage of that, right? It's only right.

Then there was the fact that I'd recently seen the Ray J episode of MTV Cribs, and apparently he was living in a bedroom in his sister Brandy's house, well into his 20s. I don't even think it was a Ray J episode of Cribs. It was probably a Brandy episode, and they figured they'd get a look at the room Ray J was living in. You know, since they were already there. He was marginally famous himself, Brandy having gotten him a job on that show on the WB she was on. Ray J had a keyboard in his room, and he played some music he was working on. It didn't sound like he could have a successful career in music. Hence, presumably, this career as a guy who takes advantage of having a famous sister to become a prolific defiler of women.

I don't think I need to tell you where this is headed. My post about hunting down and putting an end to Kanye West's mother—jokingly, of course—became the template for my post about hunting down and putting an end to Ray J. Okay, so maybe this one was a bit more graphic. What can I say? I was frustrated. I fantasized about taking him up on the roof of that house he shared with Brandy, removing his trashstache with a circular saw and tossing him over the side. There was also some talk about the rumors of his many romantic conquests. That was of course the justification for dropping him from the roof.

It wasn't until a while later that my site disappeared from the Internets. I was at my parents' house, probably looking for something to eat, and I figured I'd use one of their laptops to make sure my blog was still on the Internets. Bloggers spend a lot of time clicking refresh on their own blogs to make sure they're still on the Internets. 99.9% of the time this is silly, compulsive behavior—like spending all day and night on Twitter, but arguably less pathetic. This is the .1% of the time when someone's blog actually wasn't on the Internets. Namely, my own blog.

I clicked refresh like a million times, in case the button was sticking or something (I don't claim to know how these things actually work), but to no avail. My shit had somehow disappeared. I was able to access the software I used to publish it, but I couldn't figure out a way to bring it back. It had somehow been blocked, like the Illuminati was trying to play games with my life. Imagine having wasted so much of what could have been the most productive years of your life goofing around on the Internets, only to not have anything to show for it. Talk about an existential crisis.

Finally, I was able to pull it up using an alternate, generic domain name, the kind they give you for a free blog on, say, Blogger or Tumblr. So it must have been a problem with the domain name. I purchased the domain way TF back in '02, when I first had the ambition, if not the actual drive, to move beyond copying and pasting things I found in my email and on other websites. I locked it down for a year or maybe two years, however much I could afford at the time. And then when it came time to renew it, because my blog was the only thing that was going even kinda right with my life at that point, I renewed it for quite some time. I don't even think I've had to renew it since, and this is 2012. It couldn't have been expired. It must have been broken.

One problem: When I purchased it, and then again when I renewed it, I used this email address that I wasn't using anymore. It was through Netscape, if you can imagine. I only signed up for it because it seemed to be the easiest thing to sign up for, and I didn't want to use my college email address, because I was damn near out of college. I had long since moved on to something else. I couldn't access the site I used to purchase the domain name without the password, and I couldn't get the password without being able to access the old email address.

I lucked out in that the password I needed to access my old email address was the same password I'd been using since the 1990s, 1234. But once I finally cracked that bitch open, come to find out they'd deleted all of my old email. I guess they couldn't afford to just store it, because they were Netscape, so how were they gonna get the money? What do they even sell? My old email? But I *was* able to get the domain registrar to email a new password to the Netscape address. It arrived, and I used it to log into the domain registration website. Nope, my name hadn't expired. I used a handy form to send a message to their help department. In India, I'm sure.

Apparently, they had been forced to remove my site from the Internets, because they sent me an email saying I had to remove my post about Ray J by a certain date and I hadn't responded to it. Now it all made sense. I did recall receiving an email about how I had to remove the Ray J post—but not from the domain name company, from the blogging software company. I guess Ray J's people had contacted both of them. I got the email from the blogging software company, and I went ahead and just deleted the damn post. They said I didn't have an option, because it's illegal to threaten to kill people via the Internets. I could have tried to argue that it was clearly meant as a joke, but I figured it wasn't worth it, because it was Ray J. Anyway, anyone who wanted to read that post had long since read it. I'd made my point.

So the domain name company had my blog removed because of a post that wasn't even there anymore. I had complied with Ray J's people's request, I just didn't reply to the domain name company letting them know that I had, because I didn't get the original email from them about it, because I wasn't using that email address. What a mess.

Fortunately, it wasn't too much hassle getting my site back on the Internets, once I was able to explain what had happened. It did take a day or two after they flipped the switch in order for it to actually show up again. That didn't make any sense to me. You would think that information, once it's made available via the Internets, should be accessible almost instantaneously. There must be some guy who has to sign off on it. Anyway, I thought my problems having to do with Ray J had come to an end. Little did I know.

I was reminded of Ray J's attacks on free speech when I stumbled upon the work of a woman named Gina McCauley. She ran a blog called What About Our Daughters that became famous for a few weeks back in the mid to late '00s for its efforts to deny people their right to say whatever they'd like to say on the Internets, TV, the radio, and various other forms of media. CB radio. Pamphlets. Comic strips. You name it, she wanted to censor it.

She had come to prominence along with the movement against BET. I don't think she was actually part of that movement, but she rode the wave of publicity generated by people bitching and moaning about BET, for a variety of reasons. There were feminist types who were against explicit rap videos like Nelly's infamous "Tip Drill" video, which included a scene with the rapper swiping a credit card down a woman's ass crack, like he was making a purchase, because they were degrading to women, but there were also older religious freaks who were against rap videos because they didn't want any ass cracks exposed in music videos, period. It's the same dichotomy you find in Lupe Fiasco's views on how women are depicted in rap videos.

Some of the religious nuts would regularly protest outside the house of the black lady who was nominally in charge at BET, not unlike Anonymous' famous protests against $cientology. Then one of them got the bright idea to figure out the address, in New York, of the CAC who actually owns BET. That actually got them in the paper.

Gina McCauley's shtick involved taking attacks on the ego and trying to conflate them with attacks on the person. She would do is take two separate incidents, like a comedian calling a mostly-black girls college basketball team ugly on a late night TV talk show, and a vicious alleged gang rape, and try to make it seem as if the one had anything to do with the other. If someone, somewhere, said something that could be viewed as offensive black women, so the thinking went, they lacked respect for black women, and lack of respect for black women is what leads to horrific crimes against black women. End jokes about ugly girls basketball players, end vicious gang rape. It was kinda brilliant, but it was also kinda retarded.

With that kind of Steely Dan-style pretzel logic as her justification, she would scan the media like a hawk, looking for things that could be viewed as offensive to black women. If and when she did find something, she would use her blog to launch phone and email harassment campaigns against the companies that advertised on the TV shows, websites and what have you where she found whatever it was that made her feel fat and hence threatened the lives and the... erm, chastity of millions of innocent black women. She'd have one of her minions find the private contact info of someone who worked there, and she'd urge her readers to deluge them with calls and emails until she got her way. Or their fingers got tired. Usually the latter, as far as I could tell.

Having one of my posts temporarily removed from XXL may have been her life's single crowning achievement. She was the talk of a certain corner of the Internets at the time for her campaign to continuously mention an especially unfortunate (is there any other kind?) gang rape that took place down in Florida. Literally, that was the purpose of the campaign, as far as I could tell. I figured I would mention it, since it was in the news, and use it as a jumping off point to discuss Ray J's attacks on freedom of speech. I did that a lot in my column for XXL. I'd find whatever happened to be in the news that day and use it as a jumping off point to discuss something that was more interesting to me personally. I learned from the very best—the op-ed in the New York Times, an outright cesspool of asinine pet issues.

The thing that really seemed to set Gina McCauley off was the part where I cast some doubt on the allegations in the gang rape case she loved to bring up. I didn't say that I was actually down there, fifth in line, and I knew for a fact what happened. I merely said that oftentimes these gang rape cases are actually group sex gone awry. It starts off with a chick consenting to have sex with 8 or 15 guys, in a sort of mini Houston 500, and then maybe her ladyparts get raw, from that much friction, baby, or someone finds out that she got it on with that many guys in the same day, so she has to say it was nonconsensual, to save face. I've seen it happen a million times.

And the other thing I did was use the term hooker to sorta kinda refer to the victim in the case. I didn't mean to suggest that she was definitely out there doing something strange for some change, and I don't think it comes off that way when you read it, I just suggested that theoretically she could have been. Just like theoretically I could be. It doesn't bother me to say that, because I don't have any problem with people thinking someone paid to have sex with me. As long as it's a woman. But you try talking any sense into Gina McCauley. It's useless.

If I had it to do over again, I would have left out that last part. Why give your enemy the rope to hang you with? Though I guess nothing *really* bad ever came of that post. She tried to organize a phone and email harassment campaign against New Balance, but New Balance wasn't really advertising on that page. It was Google Adsense. New Balance probably paid Google $5 to advertise on like a million pages, and that was one of them. New Balance could remove their banner from that one page and Google would just replace it with something else. XXL would still make the same peanuts per click.

The post did come down, for a period of time, but it somehow came back.

I think what happened was, they "unpublished" it, to stop people from complaining, but it was somehow accidentally republished when the site was redesigned, or when they went to publish something else. I noticed it was still there, half a decade-plus later, when I found a link to it via an article about the infamous Too Short fingerbang scandal (it's as great as it sounds, but it took place after I left). Someone pointed to it as an example of how XXL has a history of encouraging attacks on black women. If you can consider fingerbanging an attack on black women, then yeah, I do encourage attacks on black women.

Gina McCauley's career, like so many great things on the Internets, ultimately has its roots in the Imus incident. She started off pissed off at comedian DL Hughley for something he said about the girls basketball team at Rutgers University. No, he didn't suggest you try to get them up against the wall and stick two fingers down their gym shorts. God forbid. He said they were some of the ugliest women he'd seen before in his life. Which really is a very nice thing to say. I've come to agree with Gina McCauley on that.

That's regardless of whether or not you find it to be true. Because if they really are the ugliest women in the world, then it's just mean. It's like going up to a special kid and making fun of him for being special. You don't call a special kid special, you call an otherwise normal kid who's not quite as intelligent as you special. Similarly, you don't call an extremely ugly girl ugly. You call her smart, or funny. She'll get the idea. You call a slightly flawed but otherwise kinda attractive woman ugly, to break down her self-esteem, to make her more likely to have sex with you. (I hope you're writing this down.)

If those girls weren't really the ugliest women in the world, then it wasn't just mean but it was also inaccurate. There was no good that could possibly come from that statement. It was precisely the kind of conversation we so often found ourselves having in the wake of the Imus incident, when the crotchety, racist old radio host famously called the Rutgers girls basketball team nappy headed hoes. If he had it to do over again, I'm sure he wouldn't have said it, even though it only ever resulted in him receiving a free vacation and a pay increase. But what a hassle it was.

It all started with Imus commenting on video from a championship game between the girls basketball team at Rutgers and the girls basketball team at the University of Tennessee. There was a huge disparity between the skin tone of the black girls on the Rutgers team and the black girls from Tennessee, and hence, to racists, the girls' perceived beauty. The girls from Rutgers were a lot darker and didn't have as "good" hair as the girls from Tennessee.

Whether this was by chance or by design was one of those things that got lost in all of the discussion of whether or not Don Imus is a racist, whether racists should be allowed to work for a living, and what role, if any, rap music played in any of this. The truth of the matter is that the black community does have a lot of hangups having to do with skin tone and race, but black people were ultimately successful in deflecting any discussion of our own problems onto Don Imus, who said a bad word.

It's a known fact that some colleges purposely select black people based on their skin tone. Some all-black colleges are for dark skinted black people, and some all-black colleges are for light skinted black people. Morehouse College, for example, is famous for allegedly forcing applicants to send in pictures of themselves holding a paper bag up to their faces as recently as the 1970s. My play cousin Killer Mike went to Morehouse. To think, if that policy had continued into the 1990s, he would have been denied an education. The album R.A.P. Music wouldn't be nearly as erudite. It would sound like Wacka Flocka.

The University of Tennessee isn't a historically black college, as far as I know, but that wouldn't necessarily stop them from purposely trying to field a girls basketball team filled with nothing but light skinted black chicks, just like in my dreams. Or rap videos, for that matter. There's only like three girls basketball teams that even try to compete for the championship year in and year out (I saw it on HBO's Real Sports), so they can afford to be extra selective. Whereas, I suspect that Rutgers can't afford to be as choosy. They just want the girls who can shoot the best hoop, never mind their looks.

I can see how seeing two teams like that go against each other would be jarring for Don Imus. Which is not to say that he was right for what he said.

I'm just saying. Anyway, it wasn't like he was personally calling the Rutgers girls basketball team nappy headed hoes. Why should he care what they look like? I don't think Don Imus is into black chicks. Not even adorable light skinted black chicks. What he meant to suggest is that black people, who are known to have issues with skin tone, hair and what have you, would find the Rutgers team less attractive than the team from Tennessee. He was trying to reference the Spike Lee film School Daze, but he couldn't remember what it's called, because he's as old as shit.

Arguably the very best moment in the entire Imus incident, which began in the mid 2000s and will continue in some form or another forever, was when Don Imus went on TV and tried to claim that he got the term nappy headed hoes from rap music. It was one of those things that was so ridonkulous you had to momentarily turn away from the TV to make sure it really happened. And then you just kinda had to begrudgingly respect it. Slick move, Don Imus, blaming your own racist bullshit on young black men. There's no way America can believe that something bad that happened didn't have to do with young black men. That's just not how America works.

Several people checked, via the Internets, and couldn't find one single instance of the phrase nappy headed hoes in a rap song. Bald headed hoes, sure, but not nappy headed hoes. I'll admit, I was kinda surprised. My natural tendency is to want to believe the worst about rap music. Like Hulk Hogan ("Ho Kogan"), I am a real American. MTV asked Snoop Dogg if he thought rap music had anything to do with it. He said that when rappers call black women bitches and hoes, they're referring to no-good women in the ghetto, not elite college girls basketball players. It was actually a very smart statement. People laughed at it because people have a hard time taking black men seriously, because of racism.

And if there was an absolute nadir in the Imus incident, it was when President Obama, who was still on the campaign trail at that point, was forced to chime in. They didn't tie him up and send in Samuel L. Jackson in the great movie Unthinkable, or anything like that, but someone asked him about it, and I guess he felt like it was a good opportunity to put some distance between himself and some of the more unfortunate elements in the black community, to set racist white voters at ease.

Bill Clinton had to pull a similar move in the 1992 election. I think white people were concerned about his relationship with Jesse Jackson. Later, when Clinton didn't have to sweat running for office again in his life, Jesse Jackson was his spiritual adviser during the Monica Lewinsky scandal. Then come to find out Jesse Jackson had a jumpoff of his own and an outside kid, as its known in the black community. White people may have had good reason to be concerned about Clinton's relationship with Jesse Jackson.

And so Clinton famously assuaged white voters' fears by throwing obscure community organizer and Public Enemy weed carrier Sister Souljah under a bus, in what became known as the very first Sister Souljah moment. Souljah had very reasonably, I think, suggested that black people who stay killing other black people take a week off to kill white people. Let white people see how it feels to be constantly at risk of being shot, and maybe we could get some real crime prevention, not just the BS prison-industrial complex. She wasn't advocating killing people per se. But as long as people were getting killed anyway, we might as well spread it around some, no? Black people would still be getting killed 51 weeks out of the year.

Some young guy at a campaign rally, who was probably planted there by Obama's staff, asked the candidate what he thought about rappers constantly referring to black women as bitches and hoes, causing Don Imus to not be able to come up with anything better to say in discussing a college girls basketball game and thus possibly leading to a vicious gang rape. Obama said that he found rap lyrics to be degrading to women, and he doesn't find that inspiring. As if. Keep those two things in mind, because we will be returning to them shortly ("degrading to black women," "not inspiring").

Russell Simmons was not about to take this lying down. He was already fired up, I think for a couple of reasons. One, he had come to defense of rap music in the Imus incident, in part because he felt like it would be an easy way to get his name in the paper, and—credit where credit is due—in part because it was the right thing to do. Two, he was jealous of Obama because he may have once harbored delusions of being the first black president himself. (It seems ridonkulous until you consider the, uh, work he does in the modeling world. My self-esteem would be through the roof as well, if I were Russell Simmons.) His silly as-told-to autobiography, which I read when I was in college, seemed designed to prepare him for some sort of career in politics, despite all of the talk about spending the '80s on angel dust and the '90s balls deep in models. I guess he figured there was no way he could cover that stuff up. There's too much video evidence.

IIRC, Rush was in the tank for Hillary Clinton (if that's a correct use of the term) more or less until it was clear that she wouldn't in fact be the Democrat nominee. He may have been angling for some sort of cabinet position or kickback when she got elected, if he could swing enough of the black vote. He knew he didn't have anything coming if Obama got elected. Obama can't be seen associating with too many rappers. Rush famously called Obama a mouse, in an interview with the Times Magazine. It was maybe the most Kool Keith-like thing Russell Simmons has ever said, which is saying something, but I think I get where he was coming from. I never bought any of that BS about Obama's campaign money coming from $5 donations from schoolteachers.

Something probably needed to be done to mend Obama's relationship, as it were, with the hip-hop community. I don't know if there was ever any real risk of black people not voting for Obama in the '08 election, but why take any chances? It was arranged for the candidate to appear on the cover of VIBE magazine. Which is kinda like a rap magazine, right? It did come to be associated with the East Coast-West Coast rap beef in the mid to late '90s, which resulted in the deaths of Biggie Smalls and Tupac Shakur.

The cover story was written by Jeff Chang, who lacks credibility. He's been highly criticized by KRS-One, one of the foremost authorities on the history of hip-hop (which is something you live, as opposed to rap, which is something you do). If you ever hear the song "I Was There," or whatever it's called, from that same album with Marley Marl that caused me some problems with Elliott Wilson, a song about hip-hop historians who don't conduct sufficient research, that's about Jeff Chang. KRS-One found Jeff Chang's book Can't Stop, Won't Stop, on the history of the hip-hop generation, to be both incomplete and inaccurate. Some shit wasn't there, and some of the shit that was there wasn't true. What a crock.

I later found where Chang may have paid godfather of hip-hop Kool Herc to be interviewed, in a round about way, which is probably not considered kosher according to, uh, the rules of journalism. That doesn't *seem* like it should be allowed anyway. I read an article in New York magazine about the birthplace of hip-hop, in the Bronx, which at the time was at risk of being torn down. Residents were trying to have it declared an historic landmark. The reporter caught up with Kool Herc, who supposedly invented hip-hop in that building in 1973, but he wouldn't agree to be interviewed without first being paid. He said he didn't do interviews for free. Hmm...

I found that to be odd, since he was interviewed extensively for Can't Stop, Won't Stop. He didn't just answer a few questions over the phone, like I do from time to time when a newspaper is looking for a quote on homophobia in hip-hop, it seemed like he answered a veritable shedload of questions. I grabbed the book (which I received for free along with a review copy of a book by Touré) from my shelf and checked to see if it said where Kool Herc had been paid to be interviewed. I was then reminded that Kool Herc had "written" the foreword ("forward") to the book, for which he was presumably compensated. If only magazine articles had forewords. NY mag would have been in business.

Elsewhere in this issue of VIBE was an interview with Oprah Winfrey that hadn't even been conducted recently. It was from way back in the '90s. It didn't have any historical significance or anything, it was just old. I read it anyway, just to see what she was talking about. I have great memories of rushing home from school, in the late '90s, to watch that episode where she admitted that she used to be on crack. And wouldn't you know, this interview just so happened to touch on rap music. I was struck by Oprah's comments on rap music, because they were almost the exact same as Obama's at that campaign event. Like, to the point where she told Obama to say that. I almost squirted milk through my nose.

The idea that a black guy was running for president, and Oprah Winfrey was giving him talking points, in order to dis Ludacris by proxy, presumably in exchange for the coveted Oprah endorsement (as if) was a little bit too rich even for me. I'd seen some bizarre things in my career so to speak as a professional blogger, but this took the cake. It took me a while to even wrap my head around it.

It used to be the case that a white candidate would throw a black rapper under a bus in order to signal to racist white people that black people didn't have anything coming in the next four to eight years, as if there was ever any question. Now we've got black candidates throwing black rappers under a bus, on orders from Oprah, who has deep-seeded issues with black men, in exchange for a plug on her show, which appeals primarily to older white women. Is this what Obama meant by post-race America?

# 15 SHORT PEOPLE GOT NO REASON TO LIVE

The easiest way to make a lot of money with a rap blog is to post links to every new rap song you can possibly get your hands on for illegal downloading. It's not easy in the since that constantly scouring the Internets for new rap music at all hours of the day and night and clicking an upload button hundreds of times of day isn't time consuming, and I'm sure hard on your fingers, but it's still preferable to selling crack to schoolchildren, breaking into people's cars or whatever you'd be doing otherwise.

Nah Right invented this form of rap blogging back in 2005. Noz, my former colleague at XXL, likes to claim that eskay of Nah Right jacked his entire stizz from Cocaine Blunts, and there's some truth to that. Cocaine Blunts, Noz's old blog, would post mp3's of songs that were genuinely remarkable: regional rap no one ever heard of; demos of famous rappers who would go on to record something you'd actually want to listen to; southern rap that was especially ignorant. Nah Right's brilliant idea was to focus on new music by famous (and would-be famous) rappers. It was useful in that it could save you a lot of money. Why pay a dollar to download a new T.I. song from iTunes when you could just download it from Nah Right for free?

It was only a matter of time before there was a crackdown.

Lupe Fiasco was one of the first people to take notice, not because he's a visionary businessperson but because he's insane. He was under the impression that someone had broken into his computer, and he must have been concerned with what they would find. It couldn't have been the rap music he was concerned with, because people were going to steal it anyway, regardless of how they got their hands on it.

There must be something on his computer that Lupe Fiasco doesn't want us to know about. Could it be pr0n? A cache of interracial pr0n, like the one Kanye travels with, might upset his black female listeners. Gay pr0n would obviously be an issue. Any pr0n at all would go against his image as a Muslim with jihadist tendencies who objects to the way women are depicted in rap videos, not because it makes rap music look bad, but because he thinks there should be limits on the ways women are allowed to dress.

I remember at one point a shedload of previously unreleased Lupe material all of a sudden appeared on the hip-hop Internets. A few rap blogs posted it, claiming that someone had sent it to them, not that they hacked into Lupe's computer and stole it. Peter Rosenberg played it on his Sunday night mixshow on Hot 97, trying to pass it off as an exclusive, as if Lupe or someone at the label had sent it to him, but he'd obviously just downloaded it from somebody's blog.

That must have been what set Lupe off. Either he planned to release those songs on a mixtape, for marketing purposes, or he didn't want them to be released at all, because they weren't up to his usual high standards, and they somehow ended up on the Internets. And it could be that someone really did hack into his computer and steal them, or it could just be that one of his weed carriers emailed them out to people.

Lupe first retaliated by putting the kibosh on any of his official music that turned up on blogs like Nah Right. He could have his label send out a cease and desist, and the blogs didn't have any choice but to comply, or else the label could sue them. Or they'd probably just contact the companies that host the blogs and have them removed from the Internets remotely, not unlike what Ray J did to my blog.

This led to an hilarious series of posts in which eskay would complain that it wasn't in the best interest of the labels to not allow him to give away for free songs they could just as easily charge a dollar for on iTunes, because he was helping promote artists by giving their music away for free. In fact, many artists and artist representatives purposely send their music to Nah Right for free giveaway.

I would then respond in a post for XXL in which I'd point out that Nah Right was becoming, by definition, not worth reading, because the labels were starting to understand its scheme. Whenever Nah Right would post something that someone might actually pay money for, the labels would have it removed via cease and desist. What remained were songs that no one would possibly pay money to listen to, and in some cases, songs you couldn't pay people to listen to.

To which eskay would respond by threatening to drive all the way from the unfortunate town in New York where he lives to my native Missouri, climb up on a milkcrate and punch me in the face. But I figured I was probably safe, because he would threaten to beat Noz up twice as often as he threatened to beat me, and Noz, who's emotionally disturbed, would egg him on. He couldn't travel from New York to Missouri to attack me without bypassing Noz in New Jersey, and I think technically that would violate the code of the street. You can't just skip a state.

We went back and forth like that a few times. Things finally came to a head when Lupe put a shoe on one of the kids from 2dopeboyz backstage at a show in Las Vegas. 2dopeboyz is a member of the New Music Cartel, eskay's group of rap music piracy blogs. Meka from 2dopeboyz was one of the people I worked with at XXL, towards the end of my tenure there. The other guy from 2dopeboyz is a white guy with a lip piercing who's one of the main people rumored to have hacked into Lupe Fiasco's computer. He lives out there in Las Vegas. He went backstage I guess thinking he'd clear up this email hacking rumor once and for all. Big mistake.

eskay's response was to stop posting Lupe's music. He was already hamstrung in his ability to give away Lupe's music for free, because of the label, but I guess this way Lupe wouldn't benefit from the free publicity. He also threatened to attack Lupe—but the way it was phrased, it wasn't clear to me if he meant that he was going to beat Lupe up or if he was going to have someone else beat Lupe up or perhaps shoot him. I think he was purposely vague because he didn't want to rile Lupe up.

Lupe is in New York all the time to meet with his label and to hand out free tents at Occupy Wall Street. It would be nothing for him to schedule a meeting somewhere with eskay, not unlike Nas and 2Pac's infamous confrontation in Central Park during the height of the East Coast-West Coast beef back in the mid '90s.

The problem with running the kind of blog where you post anything and everything that turns up in your inbox is that it inevitably tends to favor the kind of people who have the time to sit around sending out email.

The very best rappers aren't necessarily spending a lot of time sitting around a computer. They might not be computer literate. Or otherwise literate. They're out here selling drugs in order to have something to write about, disrespecting women and/or making sweet, passionate love to women, doing interviews in which that say "you know what I'm saying," so on and so forth. It's a wonder they find time to record music in the first place, let alone promote it.

In the mid to late '00s, nerdy rappers like Mickey Factz, Crooked I and Freeway took advantage of this by recording new songs and sending them to bloggers to for posting once a week, once a day or sometimes seemingly once every few hours. It was a good way to generate publicity for an upcoming release, except that when your new album finally hit "stores" it didn't sell any better than if you had spent the prior month watching deep cable, eating barbecue and taking a nap.

So of course XXL turned to rappers who were heavily promoted on blogs when it came time to put together a group of artists for their annual Freshman 10 issue back in like '08. This issue was a sort of sequel to a big group cover they put out back in the mid '00s, when they must have had a lot of artists the major labels were pressuring them to put on the cover, because they weren't famous enough to warrant being featured on the cover of a rap magazine. If they were weed carriers, they could at least pose alongside the bag's proprietor. 50 Cent, for example, would sometimes appear on the cover with one of his, erm, subordinates if they had an album coming out that month. He didn't have to do that for them. I hope they appreciate that.

That '08 Freshman 10 cover was big on hipster rappers—guys in tight jeans, expensive retro tennis shoes, those Rachel Ray terrorist scarves... the only thing that was missing was the cape and the t-shirt with the picture of your own face on it. I expected these guys' careers to fizzle out over the course of several years, but most of them tragically exploded shortly after liftoff, like the space shuttle Challenger.

Half those guys I can't even remember anymore. Blu was averaging one good idea every few weeks for a couple of years leading up to being featured in XXL and hasn't released anything that I'm aware of since. I think he got signed to a major label and stuck in some sort of limbo. Curren$y has his own weed-themed album (or is it a mixtape?) of the week program. A few of them were released via a label Damon Dash was running out of an art gallery he was squatting and throwing illegal concerts in after he blew the umpteen million dollars he received after Jay-Z systematically cut him out of every business venture the two of them had entered into. I knew it was all over when I read that he couldn't make the payments on a Chevy Tahoe that ended up getting repoed. Wale lucked out and was able to become a weed carrier for Rick Ross. His original fans can't stand him, but I think a couple of his songs are popular in strip clubs.

I was all ready for Asher Roth's career to go up in flames, not because I'm racist against white people, or because I have anything against him personally (he seems like a nice guy), but because I find him to be a marginal talent and it was clear to me that his career was fasttracked because he's white and hence had the potential to be the next Eminem.

Eminem was one of the most successful rappers of the '00s and arguably the most successful rapper period. He sold more albums in the 2000s than any other artist, including country musicians, Beatles reissues and Buhweet. There hasn't been another white rapper nearly as successful, unless you want to count the Beastie Boys, which is an entirely different thing, but that's not gonna stop the major labels from trying.

At the time, Eminem was gearing up to release his first big comeback album, Relapse, the one no one really cared about. Signing a young white rapper in 2009 made good business sense, because they could benefit from the hype generated by the reemergence of Eminem, not unlike how a lot of long since forgotten white rappers got (lucrative) major label deals after that first Eminem album blew up back in the late '90s.

Hence Asher Roth was one of the first people from that second XXL Freshman 10 cover, with all of the hipster rappers on it, to release an album on a major label. Some of those people still haven't put out albums. Asleep in the Bread Aisle was set to hit stores that spring. Asher Roth set out on a tour of college campuses to promote its release.

I let loose with a number of posts, mining the situation for as many lulz as I could. I was even invited to write something for Gawker, which rarely if ever publishes anything written by black people. I think the only two black people to ever post there are myself and TAN, the guy who let me post something there, on the weekend, when no one was looking. All of the other references to me there are decidedly negative. I of course predicted that Bread Aisle wouldn't be any good and that no one would buy it.

Then the shit hit the fan. Asher Roth said something very offensive on Twitter. He was in New Jersey to play a show at Rutgers University. He couldn't update his Twitter as often as he usually could, when he was just sitting around playing with his computer. (I felt the same way when I was at White Castle.) His album was coming out that week, and you really should try to be on Twitter as often as possible the week your album is coming out, for marketing purposes.

He took to Twitter to apologize for not being on Twitter, and in doing so he made reference to Don Imus' infamous remarks about the girls basketball team at Rutgers.

Asher Roth's tweet was something to the effect of, "I'm sorry I can't be on Twitter today. I'm enjoying a day of rest and relaxation hanging with nappy headed hoes." LOL

Right away, several people screencapped it and posted it on their blogs. I screencapped it and posted it on my own blog. This was back before screencapping and posting tweets was an easy content solution for lazy bloggers. Mary J. Blige would say something ridiculous like, "Why do people understand estimate my intelligents?" and it would be lost to the dustbin of history.

In retrospect, I can see why people were so upset with Asher Roth, though of course it was my natural tendency to jump to his defense at the time, both as a free speech issue and "for my own personal amusement." The term nappy headed hoes doesn't sound that bad, if you're a guy with hardly any hair on his entire body except for a thin but classy mustache. It's actually kinda funny. It's got a nice ring to it. I'm surprised Imus came up with it. But you know how black women are about their hair. The fact that most black women don't have very good hair bothers them more than things that actually should bother them. If Imus had said that the Rutgers team weren't very good students, it wouldn't have been nearly as much of an issue.

In situations like this you have to set aside the fact that something probably shouldn't be viewed as offensive (e.g. Asian people who don't want to be seen as being good at math) and just accept that it is. That is, if you're at all concerned with offending people. My problem with Asher Roth is that he didn't have the balls to stand by his statement. I'm not saying he should have doubled down on trying to purposely offend black women. He should have just explained what he meant by the joke and been done with it. If people were still offended at that point, that's their problem. Instead, he let his handlers talk him into deleting the tweet, as if it didn't happen, and as if it hadn't been captured for posterity all over the place, and going on an ill-advised apology press tour which resulted in him putting his foot in his mouth again, with some weird comments about Africa, or as he likes to call it, the motherland.

In the meantime, a separate and yet related controversy was a brewin', having to do with the fact that Nah Right didn't see fit to post anything having to do with Asher Roth's and the resulting PR crisis. It was alone in that sense. Literally every other blog on the Internets was goofing on Asher Roth. Many people felt that Nah Right was under pressure, perceived if not outright, to not post anything negative about Asher Roth. And by many people I mean many people, not just myself. Because sometimes I'll use a phrase like "some people think" as an excuse to inject my own opinion into an article, the way it's done in real journalism, but in this case I don't recall being one of the main people—or at least not the only person—to get on eskay's case about his suspect coverage of Asher Roth. Even people who read Nah Right on a regular basis and post in the comments section there could sense that something was amiss. That's when you know something is amiss.

Sites like Nah Right were instrumental in the rise of shitty late '00s hipster rappers like Asher Roth. If one of them were to blow up, Nah Right would suddenly be thrust into the position of Al Sharpton-like kingmaker. The tall Israelis who run rap music almost certainly would take notice. For Nah Right to accurately report on Asher Roth's racist comments would be like the mid '00s-era XXL throwing 50 Cent under a bus. But aside from just the ethical/business considerations, there was a race element. A black media organization providing cover for a white artist's negative comments about black women would be beyond the pale even by online hip-hop standards. That would be like Jet magazine coming to Elvis' defense that time he said his background singers showed up late because they were backstage eating watermelon, or whatever he's alleged to have said.

I'm assuming that eskay realized this, and that's why he eventually "banned" Asher Roth from Nah Right pending an apology (very Al Sharpton of him), more so than anything I said. It's not in his nature to acquiesce to my demands, regardless of how right I am.

And then there's Charles Hamilton. There wasn't any one bad thing that happened to Charles Hamilton. It was a series of incidents, each one more bizarre than the last. It's an ongoing saga that could be taking a turn for the worse as I write this.

Where to begin? That time he got punched by a girl during an impromptu rap battle after revealing that he talked her into having his abortion, Fight Club-style? I guess that's as good a place as any, though that's not the beginning. I'm not even sure what the beginning would be. That time he decided to become a producer, and it turned out he just borrowed some other guy's beats from MySpace? I remember a few rap blogs got pissed at him because he promised them exclusive mixtapes, then he yanked one of them at the last minute to give it to 50 Cent's fake blog. I can't say I was upset. In fact, I kinda like Charles Hamilton. It's possible that he's brought more enjoyment to my life than any other rapper of his generation.

The girl who coldcocked him, who came to be nicknamed Knuckles, turned out to be Mary J. Blige's stepchild, though they might be estranged. Knuckles appears to be all of about 12, but she's probably old enough that Mary J. Blige isn't obligated to give her any money, if she ever was. Throughout her career, Mary J. Blige has dealt with substance abuse issues that probably aren't over despite the many songs and albums about how they are. And this girl obviously is insane. That must have been one hell of a conversation at the dinner table.

If Charles Hamilton thought there was a way he could get some money from Mary J. Blige, I don't think he would have talked Knuckles into having his abortion. He's crazy, but he's not that crazy. That must have been the source of tension in their relationship. In the video of the incident, it looks like a guy from one of those hood DVDs caught them walking down the street and asked them to spit a few bars. He probably asked Charles Hamilton, but she volunteered. She recited what sounded like a poem she'd written about the state of their relationship. Then Charles Hamilton responded with a freestyle verse in which it was revealed what she was really upset about. And the rest, as they say, is history.

Except that was hardly the end of it. It gets worse. The thing that really ruined Charles Hamilton's career, the proverbial straw that broke the camel's back, was when it looked like he somehow talked Interscope into releasing his album (though who knows if he actually did) and he announced that it had been produced by the late, great (actually dead) J Dilla via séance. No really, that's what he said. As if I could make something like that up...

Again, I think Charles Hamilton gets a bad rap. I think the idea was to donate a portion of the album's proceeds, after (theoretically) the label recouped what it cost/what they charged him to produce it, to J Dilla's poor mother and his children, who were left buried under a pile of medical bills after he died back in '06. Several unscrupulous promoters, producers, rappers and what have you proceeded to throw "tribute" parties, put out merchandise, rap over his beats and release projects in his name without cutting a check to his estate. It was one big, sad free for all.

And now here comes Charles Hamilton, claiming to have communicated with Dilla via séance. I can see why Dilla's family was upset. That's just weird. Even if it was a joke. I think Charles Hamilton was upset that he tried to do something nice for the family of one of his favorite producers, who died tragically, and it blew up in his face, and that was the best thing he could think to say in that moment. He's genuinely crazy. One time he completely forgot how to walk and he had to be rolled around in a pink wheelchair. He needed someone with some sense to help guide him through that situation, and apparently all he had was Mary J. Blige's wacky stepdaughter.

Shortly thereafter it was announced that Charles Hamilton had been dropped from Interscope like a bad habit, and that his album would never be released, not even at the end of the year, for tax purposes. Charles Hamilton immediately went into hiding from which he's never quite completely emerged. Every now and again he'll turn up on Twitter or YouTube in order to announce that he may or may not have both AIDS and cancer at the same time or to randomly dis one of the subsequent XXL freshmen, for old time's sake. Once, there was a video of him stumbling into a barbershop in a pink skullcap and challenging one of these guys who's more of an insult comic than a rapper per se to a freestlye battle. Of course he lost. I guess at least he's walking again.

# 16 ADDITION BY SUBTRACTION

Elliott Wilson just kinda up and got fired from XXL one day in 2008. I heard it was on his birthday and he had to be escorted from the building by security, but I can't confirm whether or not any of that is true.

There was a lot of misinformation having to do with Elliott being let go from XXL, and the few people in the know either weren't allowed to talk, or they didn't want to run the risk. I was told to not mention it. I didn't, at least not outright, until the guy who told me not to was let go himself, and I essentially didn't have a boss for a rather lengthy period of time. It may have been as long as six months. Finally they hired someone, but whoever it was I never really dealt with other than an initial explaining that I had a new boss. Then that person would get let go or shifted to a different department, and I'd have another "boss" for a few weeks. One time a guy emailed me to tell me that there wouldn't be anyone in the office for a few weeks, because they were running a double issue that month, and not to say or do anything out of line. It was nothing for me to call his bluff.

I speculated that management may have found some cocaine in Elliott Wilson's desk, and that wasn't allowed in the XXL offices. His monthly letters from the editor always read like the work of someone who'd just had a bump. But either I asked him or someone else asked him, and he said he never tried cocaine a day in his life. He seemed genuinely sincere about, not like he was concerned that his mom or a future employer might read it and think he had a drug problem. It didn't make sense to me why someone would make that much money, live in Manhattan, write about rap music for a living and never try cocaine... over and over and over again. How tragic is it that he suffers from high blood pressure, has to take pills that make him piss constantly and play basketball with senior citizens, and apparently it's just from having a bad attitude?

He did another one of those media tours not unlike that time XXL put out a CD compilation of recently somewhat popular rap songs. Maybe he thought someone from another magazine would read it and offer him a job. Why didn't I think of that when I got let go from XXL? That's why I'll never get anywhere in life. One of the articles I read suggested that while Elliott Wilson no longer has a job with XXL, he still has a small stake in the company. I doubt that that's true. Part of the reason why the people from The Source who founded XXL ended up leaving after a year or so was because the white people who own XXL wouldn't give them an ownership stake. I don't know if that's why they said that the people who own XXL are racists, but I'm sure it's related.

I've thought about this for upwards of an hour over the course of the past four years now, and I think the real reason Elliott Wilson was let go from XXL is because the people who owned it were trying to cut costs after the economy blew up in 2008—though this may have been before the banks all went insolvent and Congress was forced to use tax payers' dollars to bail them out under the threat of martial law from the Illuminati. They still stood to save a lot of money. At some point, it must have occurred to them that they could let go of Elliott Wilson, not replace him with anyone at all, and pocket the ridonkulous sum I'm sure they were paying him.

The first month or two after he was let go, they somehow managed to put out a magazine without an editor in chief. I guess all an editor in chief does is write that silly letter at the beginning of the issue? I don't know how magazines work, despite having worked for one for five years. Then one of the guys from King magazine, which had either gone out of business or was on its way out of business, was brought over as a sort of temporary black nominal figurehead, to maintain appearances. They may have been concerned with how it would be received if they just promoted one of the white chicks who already worked there, which is what they ended up doing a few months later.

There was this period in between when Elliott Wilson announced that his next move would be to become a professional blogger (heh) and when his blog RapRadar a/k/a RapPravda was launched that seemed to last way longer than it would take to set up a blog. You don't really have to "set up" a blog. You just have to choose which free software you want to use, enter you email address, click through a few screens and that's about it. The whole process shouldn't take any more than about 15 minutes, even if you're completely computer illiterate and you have to have the special guy from my high school library's computer lab walk you through every step of the process.

RapPravda was something ridonkulous like a full year in the making. I was concerned, because I'm a conceited person and I didn't like the idea that he was gonna come up with something way better than my blog and I'd look like a sucker. I thought he was spending that time coming up with something amazing that would blow the Internets away with the quality of its design and its content, not just a weird-looking Nah Right clone that runs a lot of banner ads for Eminem manager and RapPravda secret owner Paul Rosenberg's various business interests.

Some young guy was able to hack into RapPravda in its developmental stage and pass along to me some of its brilliant content. The blog itself had yet to be made public, but for some reason it was already publishing an RSS feed. I added it to Google Reader, and took a look at some of the posts from the beta version of RapPravda. One was a press release announcing that Soulja Boy planned to visit Niagara Falls (no, really), presumably to have sex with Brian Johnson's girlfriend, copied and pasted verbatim. I want to say that another one was just a buncha pictures of Chris Brown, but at the same time I don't, because that seems kinda gay, and I wouldn't want to accidentally accuse someone of something kinda gay.

It was also brought to my attention that RapPravda is secretly co-owned by Eminem's manager Paul Rosenberg. You might remember him from those skits from those Eminem albums from a million years ago, back when Eminem was about something. If you did what's known as a whois search on RapPravda's domain name, it turns up the name and address for Paul Rosenberg's artist management company. Note that there was no mention of Elliott Wilson, and that it wasn't registered under the name of, say, a joint company belonging to the two of them. But it could be that the two of them both own the company. They just keep it at Paul Rosenberg's house.

It's a brilliant idea, starting website secretly co-owned by a guy like Paul Rosenberg, who's capable of funneling money into it from the ad budgets at both Interscope Records and SiriusXM. He doesn't have to sweat trying to sell ad space to someone else, he can just sell it to himself, using those companies' (I'm sure seemingly infinite) money. It almost seems too easy, like it would constitute a conflict of interest, but I guess it doesn't. Jimmy Iovine would have put the kibosh on it a long time ago, if he gave a shit. I know, because Combat Jack once wrote about it, that Steve Stoute, who used to work for Interscope, used to sign artists to that label in exchange for a substantial kickback, and that may or may not have to do with why he's now an expert on post-race America.

Any mention of Paul Rosenberg seems to set Elliott Wilson off, much more so than anything you say about him. I guess he can't have people talking shit about his tall Israeli benefactor. That's smart. I don't think they want people to know that Paul Rosenberg secretly owns RapPravda. If you check the RapPravda site, under the "about me" tabs, the contact info and what have you, you can't find any mention of him. That might look weird, with as many Eminem ads as they run. When RapPravda finally launched, I was waiting to see if they would recuse themselves from covering Eminem, or if any and all posts on Eminem would carry a disclaimer. They didn't, and they didn't.

One time MTV put together one of those silly lists of the hottest MCs in the game and Eminem wasn't on it. People weren't feeling that Relapse album, which was out at the time. People weren't really feeling Recovery either, but it sold more records than Elvis and the Beatles combined because it was very popular in white rural areas, possibly having to do with meth. RapPravda let loose with a post about what a travesty this was. There wasn't any mention of the fact that the guy who owns RapPravda stands to benefit financially if MTV lied and put Eminem on that list. It was amazing.

Like when Don Imus used jiujitsu to make it seem as if rap music caused him call girls basketball players nappy headed hoes, I was disgusted by it, but I also kinda had to respect it.

I think it was at that point that Elliott Wilson made a YouTube of himself in a hotel room, clearly agitated, calling me "fuckboy" over and over and over again. No homo. It was one of the more surreal moments of my life. I wish it was still on YouTube. It got removed when one of Elliott's accounts was deleted for piracy. He's always getting kicked off of Twitter and YouTube for posting people's music for illegal downloading, to generate more traffic to RapPravda, so they can scam more money from Interscope and SiriusXM. They don't have to sweat getting permanently removed from the Internets, like OnSmash and dajaz1 (whatever that is), because Paul Rosenberg can always call someone from the Illuminati and get it all cleared up.

The other great A/V artifact having to do with my exposure of RapPravda is a voicemail message Elliott Wilson left on this guy Bucky Turco's phone begging him to delete this screencap of an email that had Paul Rosenberg's email address on it. He said something to the effect of, "You can say or do whatever you want to me, but I can't have my boss' email address posted on the Internets." Turco, an unsung blogging legend (for what it's worth), had screencapped an email Elliott sent Paul Rosenberg asking him for an Eminem song that RapPravda could post as an exclusive, as if Eminem sent it to RapPravda because it's a worthwhile media outlet, not because it's essentially his own personal propaganda organ.

It was a fascinating glimpse into how the sausage is made, so to speak, at the world's most corrupt rap website (which is saying something). And it was all the more ironic, because RapPravda had recently taken to posting people's contact info and threatening to harm people's children. Real sociopath shit. I think one of the guys who works there is a juvenile delinquent that Elliott Wilson keeps around to make himself feel more authentically black. One time this kid tried to write an article, and it was all about how he hates J Dilla. It was the most unfortunate article in the history of hip-hop journalism, far exceeding anything in my oeuvre.

So long, VIBE magazine

When I graduated from college my mom gave me a few of those white cardboard file boxes filled with magazines that had shown up to the house while I was out in East Bumblefuck. They were all Rolling Stone and VIBE. I used to subscribe to The Source, back in the mid '90s, but I let it run out, because I was strapped for cash and I was no longer as interested in rap music.

I started subscribing to Rolling Stone around the same time. The first issue I ever bought was the one with Diddy on the cover a few months after Biggie Smalls was assassinated. I remember reading a brief article on how Jeff Buckley had drowned in the Mississippi River, supposedly by accident, swimming during a break from recording the follow-up to Grace, and thinking I need to get up on this.

I got Rolling Stone in the mail for years and years, but I think I only paid for it once and they just kept sending it. Sometimes they'd send a notice saying that my subscription was about to expire again and I would only receive two more issues. As if I gave a shit. I hardly ever read any of those magazines. Every month was either some old artist I didn't give a shit about or some teeny bopper I didn't give a shit about. Only the politics section was consistently relevant.

Pretty much the only issue of VIBE magazine I ever read was the first one I ever bought, when I was on vacation with my parents in Minnesota. The Wu-Tang Clan was on the cover, and this was back when the Wu-Tang Clan was about something. It may have been the most extensive feature on the Wu-Tang Clan before they lost the plot. I was impressed. When we got back to St. Louis, I had my old man send in a check. (I still had to pay for it, but that was before I had a checking account.)

If you're at all familiar with VIBE magazine, I don't need to tell you where this is headed. Every subsequent issue I received had Brandy on the cover, or something along those lines. VIBE magazine really is the rap magazine for lames and flames. If only Russell Simmons' silly as told to autobiography had existed at that point and I had read it. In it, he explains how Time Warner launched VIBE magazine, with Quincy Jones as nominal black figurehead, after they couldn't buy The Source. Russell Simmons was also supposed to be involved, but he ended up having to walk away, and that may have been when Quincy Jones got involved. Why would Quincy Jones found a rap magazine?

Russell Simmons was pissed because the main guy in charge was a gay white guy, and a lot of the other writers were either gay, white or both. As he explained in his book, he's not a homophobe or anything, many of his friends happen to be gay (I'm assuming), it's just, why would you hire a buncha gay white guys to run a rap magazines. You wouldn't hire a buncha straight black guys to run Details, now would you? Black guys can't even get a job doing things black guys are supposed to do. I'm not mad at Rush for what he did. VIBE did turn out to be lame, though I suspect it made a lot of money. Throughout its mid '90s heyday, it was able to carry ads from fancy fashion lines that wouldn't advertise in The Source. The clothes that were advertised in The Source looked ridiculous, even back then.

Fast forward about a year later. My subscription to VIBE ran out, and I guess they weren't pursuing the same strategy as Rolling Stone, juicing its subscriber stats by giving magazines away for free, so they could charge more for ads. VIBE's strategy was to pay some company to call your house once a day until you finally gave in and resubscribed. It probably didn't cost much, because those call centers are all run out of India. They could call your house every day for the next five years for less than they'd make if you actually resubscribed. It didn't matter to me, because I was in school during the day. I was like 17 years old at the time.

But then my old man got laid off from his job. He was already on edge because he was out of a job. You know how people who've known the feeling of earning a living wage (must be nice) develop an emotional attachment to their careers. It gets all tied up with their sense of identity. That's why I'm glad I haven't done shit in my adult life but sit around in my underwear surfing the Internets. VIBE magazine would call once a day and ask him if he wanted to renew, and I guess there was no technological solution to this problem. This was still back in the '90s. The most he could think to do was re-up for two years and force me to pay for it. I think I actually had to save up for a couple of weeks just to come up with that kind of money. Yes, I'm still bitter.

So it was sort of a relief to me personally when VIBE finally went out of business.

Honestly, I'm not sure how VIBE magazine got to the point where it was at serious risk of going out of business, and I didn't bother to research it, because that's not the topic of this discussion, not because I'm lazy. I wrote an entire book using two fingers. I know VIBE was once owned by a major corporation. Wonder Bros must have divested of it after the debacle that was that late night TV talk show, and after white people lost interest in the magazine. They probably didn't see it as being authentic. On a certain level, they may have agreed with Russell Simmons, though I'm sure many of them wouldn't admit to it.

By the time the mid '00s rolled around, the only paid advertisements VIBE carried were for Luster's Pink Oil Moisturizer and the US Military. And even the military didn't pay a very good rate, because they weren't necessarily interested in the kind of guy who reads VIBE magazine. (This is all speculation.) At a certain point, it was announced that VIBE went to a Tim Ferriss-style four day work week, so it could pays its employees that much less to do the same amount of work. A lot of people were laid off. There was only a small handful of people putting the magazine together. I guess at least they were working.

I don't know if they were under stress and that's why they purposely chose to antagonize the hip-hop community or what. Like a Showtime original series, they just kinda spiraled out that last year or so. They put out an issue called the Real Rap issue with Young Jeezy on the cover. I think they did that on purpose to spite me. Then they let Elliott Wilson name RapPravda the number three rap blog on the Internets. My blog either wasn't on the list or it was way down near the bottom. I hope they left it off entirely. Some kid might see that and think my blog isn't any good.

This was maybe a month or so after RapPravda had launched, and someone on the Internets pointed out that because of the ridonkulous lead time necessary to put out a magazine, RapPravda probably hadn't even been launched when the list was put together. Either Elliott's wife, VIBE editor in chief Danyel Smith, ordered that RapPravda be put on the list, and the white guy who put the list together figured he'd put it at number three, sight unseen, because if he put it any higher people might complain, or he just decided to place it there of his own volition, in hopes that it might help him avoid the next round of layoffs.

The final straw was an Us Magazine-style gossip supplement VIBE put out, a sort of dead tree version of what's known on the Internets as a bored hoodrat blog, consisting of pictures of obscure black celebrities along with snide comments about how they weren't wearing enough body lotion or whatever. VIBE was truly desperate. I heard they borrowed a shedload of money to put it out, and if it didn't sell, VIBE was going out of business. It was Danyel Smith's idea. She bragged about it on some podcast in which she ended up going off on the two poor kids who hosted it for no apparent reason. (She also used to do a podcast with Elliott Wilson in which she'd constantly order him around and tell him to shut up. It was hard to listen to.)

She arranged so that she'd receive a double salary, as both the editor in chief of VIBE and the editor in chief of Bored Hoodrat VIBE a/k/a The Most. They may have borrowed more money than they needed specifically for that purpose. It was a good deal for her. She would have made more money per week than I make in a year. It's too bad it was the worst idea ever. It sold like you could get AIDS from reading it, VIBE had to default on its loan, and that's why it went out of business.

Thanks to the magic of technology, that last, sad day at VIBE was well documented on the Internets. VIBE's creditors had private security in place at its offices, I guess to make sure no one tried to walk out with any furniture along with the contents of their desks. They probably had to sell all of that shit on eBay to try to recoup at least some of what Danyel Smith lost.

## 17 FANUTE BOL

It's never been clear to me exactly why I was let go from XXL. I did talk to a guy on the phone who explained to me that they decided to take the site in a different direction. They were getting rid of the blog section of the site altogether, and that's the only section I wrote for, so there was no need to keep me around.

But I suspect that that was BS, because they didn't revamp the site so much as they got rid of me and left the rest of the site more or less as it was. They pulled the same shit with me that they pulled with Elliott Wilson. I check the XXL website every now and again to see if it still exists, and there isn't anything going on there. It's a far cry from its '06-'07 heyday. They don't have an online strategy per se; they just have a website. I think the way it works is they just charge the same companies that advertise in the dead tree version of the magazine to advertise on the website as well, regardless of whether or not anyone reads it. It's more of a supplemental source of income than a business venture unto itself, compared to, say, Complex, which has a shedload of "content" on its website but it isn't clear if you can actually buy the magazine in stores. Do they even bother to send it out anymore?

Everyone else who ever blogged for XXL, all 30 or 40 of them, are also to blame for my tenure at XXL coming to an end and hence the death of the possibility that I could make more than $1,000 per month. Thanks a lot, guys. No but really, by the time I was let go I was either the only person still blogging for XXL or one of only a small handful. I can't remember anymore. I stopped reading other bloggers a long, long time ago. I find it bad for my writing. I was the only member of the original XXL blogging staff who stuck around to the very end, and I may have been there twice as long as anyone else. People had a tendency to burn out, and most of the people who burned out didn't burn very bright in the first place. The kind of writing that became the standard, my kind of writing, I think tends to reward people who are obsessive in nature. The little money you get paid isn't worth the amount of time and effort it takes. You have to enjoy forcing your opinion down other people's throats. No homo.

Towards the end of my time at XXL I was trying to take my writing to another level. I'm not sure how successful I was. I started writing posts that were a lot longer than my usual 800 – 1,000 words. 2,000 to 2,500 was starting to become my new norm, but at the same time it was getting more and more difficult for me to write a new post every day of the week, and I suspect that this may have been an issue. No one ever talked to me about how often I was supposed to blog, but I always wondered if they checked my blog and were disappointed if there wasn't a new post. I think some of the people who didn't last very long were let go for being lazy. Contractually, I was supposed to blog five days a week, but I was also only obligated to write something like 100 words per day. I think that was the only way the rate I was paid didn't start to resemble slavery. Anything above and beyond that was charity work. If I had it to do over again, I would have stuck with 800 words per post, five posts per week. I think that was when I was most effective.

When word got out that I'd been let go it was suspected that it had something to do with one of my very last posts, about Odd Future. Who knows if that's true or not. Odd Future is famous for its DIY aesthetic, and at the time they weren't signed to a major label, but it was a well known fact that they had powerful industry people guiding their career. For all we know, they could have been signed all along and pretending to be independent in order to seem more authentic, which is known as astroturfing. I speculated on this in my post. It's not inconceivable that someone at the label that was guiding their career read my post, called XXL and bitched about it, afraid that I might blow their cover. I also drew the obvious connection between Odd Future and juggalos. Odd Future are in fact juggalos in every meaningful way other than the fact that they aren't fans of Insane Clown Posse, as far as I know, and juggalos were having a "moment," at the time, for a number of reasons.

ICP put out that ridonkulous video in which they marveled at the magic behind everyday items such as magnets. It ended up going viral and eventually it was parodied on Saturday Night Live. That led to more interest in the Gathering of the Juggalos, the annual event in which thousands of juggalos get together in the woods somewhere here in the Midwest to do drugs, throw things at each other, and watch performances by juggalo groups, along with older legitimate rap groups. There were a few great articles about it. You probably couldn't write a bad article about the Gathering of the Juggalos. I could probably write a pretty good article about it without even going. And then there was the guy who shot Gabrielle Giffords, who was a juggalo. This was kinda glossed over in the media, but it's true. I realized it reading an article about him in the New York Times, in which one of his friends said he was obsessed with magnets. The Times probably didn't know to put one and two together.

My article on Odd Future, black juggalos, did in fact disappear from the XXL website. It was the last such article during my time there. I'd say I went out on a high note. It was always stupid when someone from the XXL offices would go in and delete something I'd written a few hours after I published it. Inevitably, someone on Twitter would notice that it was gone, they'd find a copy of it in Google's cache or somewhere and post it on their own blogs, and it would be a lot more widely read than if they just left it alone. I guess by deleting it altogether they could prove to whoever ordered them to delete it that they really were with the program. They were always concerned with maintaining access to artists for the dead tree version of the magazine. A month or two after I was let go, for example, there was a big spread on Odd Future.

They would always do these features on Shyne, and I'm not sure why. They would fly people to foreign countries to interview him, because he wasn't allowed back in the US. I think once they got an exclusive interview with him after he went to prison for shooting the club up, and it sold well. That was a long-ass time ago. I can't imagine any of the subsequent covers sold nearly as well, but who knows. I did a few posts on Shyne towards the end there, after he emerged from prison an absolute buffoon. He converted to Judaism and forgot how to rap. But he insisted on continuing to pursue a career as a rapper. I guess because people were still willing to pay him. I don't know if he's threatening to kill people or what. Towards the end there, I went looking for something else I had written and I noticed that someone had gone through and edited seemingly everything I had ever written about Shyne to the point that it was meaningless.

Towards the end there, they stop calling or emailing me to inform me that I'd been censored. I think what happened was, they kept hiring and getting rid of people, and the new people weren't familiar with the process. The word would come down from above that something I'd written had to be censored, and they'd just go in and delete it. I wouldn't even know unless someone brought it to my attention. Also, they started deleting my posts altogether. It used to be they'd just set them to draft, so they were still saved on the site's back end, they just weren't published. I always figured I'd go back and retrieve all of my posts that had been removed for whatever reason. If XXL didn't want to publish them, I could at least publish them on my own blog, perhaps along with my theories on why they had been deleted. But if they just deleted them altogether, they were lost forever. I couldn't even save a copy for myself, to show my grandkids.

This ended up being a moot ("mute") point, both because you have to have kids in order to have grandkids and because I wasn't warned in advance when I was let go. One day I went to write a post, and my login didn't work. I emailed the last guy who had emailed me claiming to be my boss, and he replied that I'd been fired. Literally, that's how I was fired, after having worked there for a full five years and written over a thousand posts and a million words I wasn't allowed to write a farewell post or anything.

Here's Where the Story Ends

You would think that as one of the most famous hip-hop bloggers of all time, the progenitor of the form, the source of many an unfortunate trend, I would have found another opportunity to write about rap music for money, after I was let go from XXL. And you would be mistaken.

I couldn't work for any of these rap websites, because I don't think any of these rap websites actually pay people. Even XXL I don't think paid very many people who wrote for the website other than myself. Of course I wasn't allowed to discuss pay with any of my coworkers, supposedly because some of them weren't getting paid as much as I was. I think a lot of the rest of the content there was written by unpaid interns, dumbass kids trying to launch a career in journalism.

There were only about three rap magazines left. And that's a generous estimate. Sometimes The Source would go a month or two without a publishing a new issue. They were always notorious for not paying. When it was bought by the people who currently own it, it was arranged so that they didn't have to pay any of the many, many people who wrote things for The Source over the years and didn't get paid for it. Sucks to be them.

VIBE was out of business for a period of time, and then it came back. Some company bought the brand name for eight dollars and a ham sandwich. The new VIBE, which I've taken to calling Zombie VIBE, doesn't seem altogether different from the old VIBE, which means that they probably don't have any use for me. Of course I would take the money, if they were offering, but I don't think they would publish an article about anything I could write about, and I'm not sure what's the status of their website. Either it's not high on their list of priorities, or there's a capability deficit.

Though it isn't a rap magazine per se, Complex runs a lot of rap-related content and it has a very active website. I haven't seen the print version of it in a store since like 2006. But there's no way I could work for Complex, both because I suspect that some of the kids there have a problem with me personally, if you can imagine, and because they're in cahoots with a lot of the people I've had to expose over the years, including Kanye, Elliott Wilson and Paul Rosenberg.

I called Combat Jack to see if he knew of anything, and he suggested this site he worked for for like two weeks after he left XXL, a few years ago, because they weren't paying him on time. At the time, he told me they paid something ridonkulous like twice what XXL paid, i.e. something dangerously approaching a living wage. But then I don't think anyone ever worked there for more than a few weeks. Hopefully they prorate. The site didn't seem to be very active at this point. I ended up talking to the guy on the phone, but nothing really came of it. It was way early, like 6 AM on a Saturday. He had probably been up all night. I had to be up that early for my job in retail.

Combat Jack had recently become the managing editor, the guy in charge of hiring people, at The Source, but I didn't even go there, because I knew it would be a problem with the two of us working for the same company. The Illuminati might find out and have the entire building torn down.

The year before, I cost Combat Jack a job at SiriusXM. He had been hired as a co-host for the morning show on Eminem's Shade45. The girl who hosted the show explained to Paul Rosenberg that Combat had once written a few things for my blog. That's how he got into blogging. And so Paul Rosenberg kicked him to the curb before he could even begin. Damn.

I felt horrible. Not only was I out of a job myself, I was costing other people jobs. I'd become the most reviled, unemployable person in all of hip-hop. You'd think I had actually done something wrong. Meanwhile, all I ever did was crack a few jokes on the Internets. R. Kelly routinely makes love to children, and he's never been so employed.

If that's what hip-hop journalism is like, then I'm not sure if I want to work in hip-hop journalism anyway. Er, professional hip-hop journalism. I'll always have my blog, at least until the Illuminati somehow finds a way to have it removed from the Internets again, this time for good.

I'm actually less concerned with *where* I work than I am with how much money I can make. Working part-time in retail along the little money I make from my own blog just isn't cutting it. My plan now is to become an author. I want to write books. I figure this way I can continue the important work I was doing at XXL (don't laugh) and hopefully make more money than I could make just blogging. This book is the first step along that path.

I believe it was Confucius who once said that a journey of a thousand miles begins with alienating yourself from an entire industry.

# ABOUT THE AUTHOR

My government name is Byron Crawford, though many people on the Internets call me Bol, which is Swahili for "The Gulliest One." As you can see, I take no small amount of pride in my African heritage. When I'm not working like a Hebrew slave at a series of soul-crushing minimum wage jobs, I devote most of my free time to doing community outreach with black and Latino youth. No homo.

I run a website (perhaps you've heard of it) called ByronCrawford.com: The Mindset of a Champion, in which I educate today's youth on some of the most important issues of our time, including racism, homophobia, healthy living, respect for women, tolerance for religion, and who really runs the music business.

A committed feminist, I also donate as much money as I can afford to (sometimes more) to underprivileged female college students in a small, rural town called Sauget, Illinois. Because as far as I'm concerned, it's one thing to talk about it on the Internet, but it's a whole other thing to put your money where your mouth is. Literally.

I've lived in and around St. Louis, MO my entire life, except for a five year period I spent in Chicken Switch, MO. I hold a bachelor's degree in business administration, with a concentration in marketing, from East Bumblefuck State University, the Harvard of the Midwest, as well as a certificate in food safety I earned while working at a White Castle.

In addition to rap music, I'm also a big fan of the album New Miserable Experience by the Gin Blossoms. It even says so in the album's Wikipedia entry. (Note that I didn't do that myself.)

Made in the USA
Lexington, KY
21 May 2014